TOO YOUNG TO DIE

AN ASIAN PERSPECTIVE ON YOUTH SUICIDE

B. H. CHIA

TIMES BOOKS INTERNATIONAL
Singapore • Kuala Lumpur

Published by Times Books International
an imprint of Times Editions Pte Ltd
Times Centre
1 New Industrial Road
Singapore 536196
Fax: (65) 285 4871
Tel: (65) 284 8844
e-mail: te@corp.tpl.com.sg

Times Subang
Lot 46, Subang Hi-Tech Industrial Park
Batu Tiga
40000 Shah Alam
Selangor Darul Ehsan
Malaysia
Fax and Tel: (603) 736 3517

Printed in Singapore

ISBN 981 204 998 3

Contents

Acknowledgements

First, I must thank Dr Cai Yi Ming and Dr Tsoi Wing Foo for reading the book and giving me their encouragement and advice.

I started writing this book but in the end it became a family project. My love and thanks begin with my wife, and my son, Dr Patrick Chia Chong Ming, and his wife, for their support throughout my project. My son especially has helped me tremendously with my computer's teething problems. My daughter, Dr Audrey Chia Wei Lin, sacrificed part of her holidays to read my book, correcting my English and giving me her criticisms and ideas on how the book should be presented. We spent many hours discussing the various issues in the book. The discussions have helped me to crystallize my thinking.

Prologue

One would think that the young would have every reason to want to live. Yet, under certain circumstances, they have felt that they had no choice but to commit suicide. Why?

This book tries to examine this issue.

To begin the journey to understand this truly tragic but increasingly relevant phenomenon, particularly in today's troubled times, here are three suicide letters written by young suicide victims in Singapore. These perhaps illustrate best the thinking and the intense negative and positive feelings that accompany such acts.

1. A 21-year-old Chinese female. She jumped from a high-rise flat. She wrote:

How lovely is this world? I want to survive. It is my earnest desire to live on but circumstances oppress me, driving me to the path of desperation leading to death. Heaven! Why do you not stretch out your sympathetic hands to rescue me? I am in great agony. I die with my eyes unclosed. I want vengeance. I shall never spare the one who ruined me. Oh heaven! Why can't you give me a chance to survive? Why? Why?

Mother, I am really reluctant to leave you. Father, I beg you to forgive me for not being filial. Why can't I live on? Why do they not spare me? How lovely is this world and yet I cannot live on. Mother, in my heart you are the greatest person. You have to take care of yourself. I silently will bless you from beyond. Mother, you must forgive me. I have lots more to say but do not know how to begin.

I am a weak person. I cannot face the cruel reality of life. I have no strength to fight with my destiny. I can but run away from reality. I am in great agony. My problems are unsolvable.

I cannot make my parents happy but I instead bring them troubles and sorrow. I make them shed unworthy tears. I am completely at a loss. I have no choice.

Elder brother, I hope you will honour your parents and be filial to them. Love and take care of younger brothers and sisters and I shall rest in peace in hell. Thank you. Do not grieve for me because I am a piece of rotten wood that cannot be carved into something useful. I am useless. Take good care of yourself.

I am leaving my home forever. Take good care of yourselves.

My boss and my colleagues,
Well, you all may laugh. You all may beam with your victorious smiles. Well, you all may feel elated. You all have cherished malicious intentions against me. My death is unjustified. You all have ruined me and have caused my parents great grief and sorrow. Well, you all should be very satisfied. I want vengeance. I shall not let the matter come to a close. Oh! Why not spare me? Why oppress me?

I hate intensely. I have shed my last drop of tears. I have been subjected to extreme suffering. My reputation is wretched. Laugh! You all may laugh to your hearts' content.

2. A 20-year-old Chinese male, serving his national service. He hanged himself. He wrote:

Sweet,

I always trust and love you. I shed a tear when I write this letter. Do not forget me. Please forgive me. To me, this world is a stupid place to live in. People cheat people and people are cruel to people.

I have done a lot of stupid things myself. I have been used by many and I hate them. I have tried to turn a new leaf. I have stopped gambling and have stopped talking nonsense but people still do not think much of me.

I love one person as I have never loved before. She loves me but she also hurts me. I blame myself and not her.

Mother,

I am sorry. You have fed me for so long. I hurt you so but please do not scold me. I know how much you have suffered and how much you love me. I am really sorry. Forgive me please.

I commit suicide for the following reasons.

1. The one I love always hurt me.
2. I am unable to support my family.
3. My place of work.
4. The friends that I mix with.
5. The place that I live in.

Good-bye. Love.

3. A 24-year-old married Chinese male teacher. His wife had left him. He jumped from his high-rise flat. He wrote:

I know that suicide is a stupid and undesirable act. However, I have to resort to this course of action. Do you realize that the 'mind' of a person who has decided to commit side is fraught with complexity?

My heart aches as if it is being pierced with a thousand knives. I am in great anguish. My mood is at the lowest. I have lost all confidence. The thought of suicide has been in my mind for the past four years.

1
Introduction

Suicide is an old phenomenon and occurs in both primitive and civilized societies. People have been killing themselves since the beginning of recorded time. A common misconception held by many is that suicide was not common in primitive societies because life for the individuals in such societies was simple and less stressful.

However, in a primitive society in Southwest New Britain, New Guinea, Hoskin et al. (1969) found that the suicide rates in the village were double those found in the United States today. In this village, the ritualization, acceptance and familiarity of the suicide option as a response to a difficult life situation resulted in this high suicide rate. Everyone in the village knew how to knot the rope for hanging.

In fact, the suicidal motivations among primitive people in various parts of the world are much the same as those found in advanced societies. Revenge, a desire for reunion with a departed loved one, and escape from pain, punishment or dishonour are motives still as prevalent today.

Suicide is a very personal act. For some, it is a way of solving the problem of living or it is a way of achieving a better life and avoiding a worse one. A person commits suicide when he finds his life in this world has become intolerable, difficult and meaningless and he wants to escape from the situation.

Of all suicides, suicide of the young results in the greatest horror and disbelief for relatives and friends of the deceased. The loss of a young suicide is unnecessary, senseless, unnatural and wasteful. When suicide occurs among the young, it eliminates a potentially valuable member of the community. Thus, young suicide results in not only personal but also societal loss.

Much has been written on young or adolescent suicide in Western countries (Shaffer, 1974; Hawton and Catalan, 1987; Shafii, 1989; Hoberman and Garfindel, 1989) but comparatively very little has been written on young suicide in Asia.

In recent years, suicide rates of the young for most Western countries have increased alarmingly. Fortunately, this trend does not occur in countries in Asia such as Singapore, Hong Kong and Taiwan where there is a high Chinese population.

In any country, suicide of children under the age of 12 is extremely rare. It becomes more common only after the age of 12 (Chia, 1978 and 1981). In Singapore, in 1995, there were only 3 suicides in the 10–14 age group, 15 in the 15–19 age group, and 33 in the 20–24 age group. A study of young suicide in a small country like Singapore, therefore, would focus on those above the age of 14.

Singapore is a small island city, 23 kilometres wide and 42 kilometres long. It lies just 137 kilometres north of the equator and is strategically located in Southeast Asia. It has a total land area of 647.5 square kilometres. Though small, it has the fourth highest urban area population density in the world. Because of the shortage of land, high-rise flats were built to accommodate the population. Now about 85% of the population resides in such high-rise flats, built mostly by the government and sold to the residents at a subsidized rate.

The population of about 3 million (1995) comprises mainly Chinese, Malays and Indians, whose ancestors originated from the big countries in Asia – China, India/ Pakistan/Sri Lanka, and the Malaysian/Indonesian archipelago. Each of these ethnic groups has its own rich cultural heritage and religious beliefs and practices. The main religions in Singapore are Buddhism, Taoism, Islam, Christianity and Hinduism.

Singapore became a fully independent country in 1965, after 146 years of British colonial rule. Today, Singapore is a modern city. It is one of the most urbanized, industrialized and materialistically prosperous countries in Asia. The standard of living in Singapore is one of the highest in Southeast Asia.

The multi-racial nature of Singapore's population provides the opportunity to compare the pattern of young suicide of three different ethnic groups. All live in a small city which has undergone rapid environmental and economic changes after gaining its independence. The impact that these changes would have on the suicide rates of these three different ethnic groups would be interesting and worth investigating.

The percentage of the young in the population has fallen during the last one to two decades (Census of Population, Singapore 1957, 70, 80 and 90). Also, in a survey, it has been noted that about 60% of the residents in the 25–29 age group in the island has attained at least upper secondary and 16.5% has attained university qualifications (General Household Survey, Singapore, 1995).

Foreign companies are given attractive incentives to invest in the country. More foreign investments mean more jobs are being created. In fact, in Singapore, there is no lack of job opportunity for anyone able and skilful. Also, chronic drug or alcohol abuse is not a major problem among the young in Singapore. From this perspective, it could be hypothesized that the suicide rate for the young in Singapore will in future decrease rather than increase.

However, the recent financial turmoil in Asia may increase the suicide rates of the young in Singapore and the rest of Southeast Asia. The actual impact of this still remains to be seen as it will take a few years more before the latest suicide statistics become available.

Official suicide statistics are notoriously unreliable. The official suicide statistics of almost all countries are under-reported. In Singapore, the official suicide rate (1973) was under-reported by only 13% (Chia, 1978). Compared to many other countries, the official suicide statistics in Singapore are reliable.

In the East, there is a preponderance of female over male suicides. This has been attributed to the status of women in Asian countries. Women in Asia have less freedom – legally, socially, and culturally – than do men (Headley, 1983). However, in Singapore, we are seeing a move in the direction of greater freedom of choice for women. With this change will we see a lessening in the preponderance of female over male young suicides in Singapore in the years to come?

In Singapore, 23% of the young suicides (aged 10–24) left behind suicide letter/s. I strongly believe that we can learn much from these letters and have reproduced suicide letters extensively in this book. A small percentage of the suicide letters were written in Chinese or Indian and had to be translated into English for the coroner's inquest. Methods used for suicide vary from age to age and from country to country depending on fashion and availability. In Singapore, more and more of the young now jump to their death from high-rise flats.

Why do the young commit suicide? I have separated the causes into predisposing and precipitating factors. The predisposing and precipitating factors found in Asian countries vary from those found in Western countries because of the differences in genetic make-up, culture and social environments and expectations. A stress in one country may be less significant in another. For example, in Japan, it has been suggested that the intensely stressful preparation for the national college entrance examinations is a major factor for young suicide in that country (Igu, 1981). In Singapore, the young also committed suicide because of examination failure.

Also, in Singapore, the percentage of young suicides found suffering from affective disorder and personality disorder is much lower when compared with those found in Western countries. As in Hong Kong, the percentage of young suicide found associated with schizophrenia (a major mental illness) is high.

While suicide is infrequent among the young, when it does occur the shock and impact the suicide has over the parents can be both damaging and lasting. It is a tragedy that parents find difficult to forget (Chia 1978 and 1981).

The materials for this book were obtained mainly from:

1. Coroners' suicide case-files (1969–76).
2. A psychological postmortem study I conducted on 54 young suicides in Singapore (1974).

   Information obtained from the psychological postmortem study helped to supplement and correct the data obtained from the coroners' suicide case-files. In the psychological postmortem study, I visited the survivors and personally interviewed them.

   The study enabled me to have a better in-depth understanding of the character and personality structures of the individual suicides, their relationship with their close ones and the temporal sequence of stressful life events that led to their suicides.

3. Letters written by 86 young suicides (75 Chinese, 7 Indians and 4 Malays) collected from the coroners' suicide case-files (1969–76).
4. Information obtained from the case-files of 1,275 young patients I treated in my private psychiatric clinic in Singapore (1968–88). In a follow-up study of these patients, I discovered that 25 of them had committed suicide.

Materials from all these sources will give a more comprehensive picture of young suicides in Singapore.

The main aim of this book is to help readers understand why the young in Singapore felt that they had to commit suicide. With understanding comes better skill in evaluating suicide risk, and more importantly, in prevention. Psychiatrists, medical practitioners, psychiatric nurses, clinical psychologists, social workers, the clergy, school teachers, counsellors and parents will find this book interesting and useful.

2
Suicide Statistics

In all countries, suicide rates are under-reported for reasons such as insurance benefit, religious reasons, social stigma, guilt and malpractice problems. Also, differences in ways of reporting death, in investigating unnatural deaths, in the attitude of the particular society towards suicide, and bureaucratic problems also contribute to the inaccuracy of the official reports on suicide.

In Arabic countries (Egypt), it has been said that people prefer not to think about suicide. They wish it did not exist so as to accord with their cultural norms and expectations (Ahmed and Farouk, 1983). If suicide is not supposed to be a problem, it will therefore not be necessary to pursue energetically research on suicide in that country.

Also, in Asia, both Muslims and non-Muslims conceal suicide in order to maintain the family's reputation which affects the marriageability of their children and their social ranking within the community (Headley, 1983). In countries where laws against suicides are strict and attempted suicides are actively prosecuted by the police, as in Pakistan, suicide attempts or suicides are concealed to protect the family from interrogation and threat from the authorities (Ahmed, 1983).

In the United Kingdom, the Scandinavian countries and Singapore, despite the best efforts, there are still some cases of death in which the cause of death remained undetermined. Unintentional under-reporting may result when actual suicides are classified as accidents simply because there is not enough evidence to support a final determination of suicide. Some single-car crashes, overdoses and poisonings are actually suicides but are labelled as accidents because they are unverifiable as suicides.

Keeping good official records on death and suicide involves expenditure and manpower. Where the budget assigned to the department involved in such tasks is insufficient, there would not be proper recording and storage of relevant records.

Among some countries in Asia, it has been reported that:

1. Non-reporting of suicides in Taiwan was at a minimum. However, such reports are official and are not available to the public for research (Rin and Chen, 1983).
2. In Hong Kong, Lo (1992) reported that under-reporting appeared to be on the low side in view of the compactness of the whole territory and the thoroughness of the police investigative procedures.
3. In Japan, Tatai (1983) reported that the data on suicide collected by the police agency might be incomplete and not totally accurate.
4. In South Korea, a coroner's inquiry is not essential. Instead, a doctor's inquest is substituted for the former. Suk (1992) reported that the most reliable source of data on suicide in South Korea was derived from the National Police headquarters, which recorded all reported deaths from accident and suicide.

In Singapore, the important personnel involved in the suicide ascertainment procedure are the police inspector, the coroner and the forensic pathologist. The suicide verdict is given only after a coroner's inquest and the coroner does not pronounce the verdict of suicide unless there is positive evidence of 'suicide intent'. The coroner may classify 'probable suicide' where a doubt exists under other cause of death.

In the United Kingdom, suicide was a legal issue for many centuries. According to legal principles, the judgement of suicide must be based upon evidence considered to be 'beyond reasonable doubt'. In the Scandinavian countries, in contrast, the determination of suicide has been regarded as a public health matter to be decided by physicians on the 'preponderance of evidence', the customary basis of medical decisions. In the United States, Murphy (1992) reported that the medical examiner system has gradually replaced the coroner system in the more populous areas of the country.

The variation of suicide rates between countries may reflect the variation in the suicide ascertainment procedure rather than the real incidence of suicide (Barraclough, 1987). Thus, a comparison of suicide statistics of any two countries can only be made when all these factors have been taken into consideration.

How reliable are the official Singapore suicide statistics?

Different countries have different ways of reporting and certifying death and different ways of investigating unnatural death. Also in different countries, different personnel are involved or play different dominant parts in such investigations and certification.

Singapore and Hong Kong, being once British colonies, inherited a British system of suicide ascertainment procedure. However, even though the legal definitions of suicide are very similar in these two countries and in the United Kingdom, in practice it was found that they are interpreted differently with the Singapore and Hong Kong authorities requiring a higher level of proof of suicidal intent.

In Singapore, the coroners give doubtful cases of deaths an open verdict. Cases given the open verdict are assigned under the 'undetermined category' in the 'Reports on Registration of Births and Deaths, Singapore' which are published annually. The undetermined death is defined as 'injury undetermined whether accidentally or purposely inflicted'. In Singapore, Chia (1978) reported that about 57% of the 'undeclared suicides' (1973) were found from the 'undetermined category'. In Edinburgh, Overstone (1973) reported that the 'undetermined' deaths and not 'accident' deaths were the source of nearly all of the mis-classification.

In Singapore, the 'suicide to undetermined ratios' varied widely from year to year (table 2.1). In Hong Kong, Lo (1992) also found that the 'suicide to undetermined ratios' varied widely from 1982 to 1985. This variation was said to be due to a change of coroner.

In Singapore, to date, the coroners have not given a single case of motor vehicle accident a 'suicide verdict'. However, in a study of fatally injured drivers involved in vehicular crashes in Baltimore, Schmidt et al.(1977) reported that 1.7% of total fatal crashes were considered to have been suicide. It is relatively 'acceptable' to end one's life by driving off the road. Death would then be registered as accident rather than suicide. It would then be easier both on the family and on oneself. Accidents are therefore without doubt from time to time camouflaged suicide.

In Singapore, if the police inspectors investigating motor vehicle accidents were more aggressive in their approach towards excluding suicide, a few of such cases might have to be given a suicide verdict by the coroners.

Table 2.1: Trend of 'Suicide to undetermined ratio' in Singapore

Year	Rate: Suicide	Rate: Undetermined	'Suicide to undetermined ratio'
1969–72	10	2.8	3.6:1
1973–76	10.9	3.9	2.8:1
1977–80	10.8	7.9	1.4:1
1981–84	9.5	9.3	1:1
1985–88	13	5.9	2.2:1
1989–92	12.5	7.1	1.8:1
1993–96	12	6.6	1.8:1

Source: 'Reports on Registration of Births and Deaths (and Marriages), 1969–96'. Registry of Births and Deaths (and Marriages). National Registration Department, Singapore.
Rate is calculated as no of suicides per 100,000 population per annum.

Suicide to undetermined ratio for various methods of death in Singapore

In Singapore, the mean suicide to undetermined ratio found for the various methods of death varied widely from 0.2:1 (drowning) to 11.5:1 (hanging) as shown in table 2.2.

The mean suicide to undetermined ratio for drowning in Singapore was 0.2:1, varying from 0.1:1 to 0.4:1. This mode of death must have given the coroners in Singapore problems as in the Scandinavian countries (Kolmos and Bach, 1985).

The mean suicide to undetermined ratios for poisoning in Singapore was 3:1, varying from 5:1 to 2:1. Deaths by poisoning in England and Wales (Barraclough, 1978) and Dublin (McCarthy and Walsh, 1975) presented the coroners there with the greatest problems. In fact, it has been said

Table 2.2: 'Suicide to undetermined ratio' by method in Singapore

Year/Method	'Suicide to undetermined ratio'					
	Hanging	Jumping from high-rise flat	Cutting/ shooting	Poisoning	Drowning	Unspecified
1969–71	19:1	6:1	4:1	5:1	0.4:1	0.5:1
1972–74	36:1	6:1	–	4:1	0.4:1	0.6:1
1975–77	12:1	3:1	3:1	2:1	0.2:1	0.6:1
1978–80	9:1	2:1	2:1	4:1	0.2:1	0.1:1
1981–83	3:1	2:1	4:1	2:1	0.1:1	0.2:1
1984–86	3:1	2:1	3:1	3:1	0.1:1	0.2:1
1987–89	7:1	4:1	5:1	3:1	0.3:1	0.3:1
1990–92	4:1	2:1	4:1	2:1	0.1:1	0.1:1
1993–95	10:1	3:1	3:1	3:1	0.2:1	0.2:1
Mean ratio	11.5:1	3.5:1	3.5:1	3:1	0.2:1	0.3:1

Source: 'Reports on Registration of Births and Deaths (and Marriages), 1969–95'. Registry of Births and Deaths (and Marriages). National Registration Department, Singapore.

that the Irish coroners had to use a stricter definition of suicide for deaths caused by poisoning.

The mean suicide to undetermined ratios for jumping from high-rise flats and for cutting/shooting in Singapore were both 3.5:1. However, the mean suicide to undetermined ratio for hanging in Singapore was 11.5:1, varying from 36:1 to 3:1. This is the method which the coroners in Singapore have the least difficulty in reaching a verdict.

Suicide statistics of the young in Singapore

In Singapore, the official suicide rate (1973) was under-reported by 13% (Chia, 1978). In Edinburgh, based on extensive record search, Overstone (1973) concluded that the Scottish Crown Counsel under-reported suicide by 38%. In England and Wales, Barraclough (1978) reported that the official suicide figures might represent between a quarter and two-thirds of the actual numbers of suicides. In the United Stages, Toolan (1962), Kramer et al. (1972) and Gist and Welsh (1989) said that the actual rates of suicide might exceed published rates by a factor of two or three. Thus, compared to other countries, the suicide rates in Singapore are reliable.

Suicide of the young creates the greatest social stigma and guilt for their parents. Parents are often fearful of being labelled as 'bad parents'. Also, most people would feel that suicide of the young is 'unthinkable'. For these reasons, it may therefore be possible that more deaths of the young which really are suicides are instead registered as accidental deaths. Suicide rates of the young in all countries are, therefore, even more likely to be under-reported than suicides of other age groups.

3
Patterns and Trends

Singapore

Singapore in 1819 was a small fishing village with fewer than 200 Malay fishermen. With its independence in 1965, it began to industrialize and modernize to survive economically. It has no natural resources but it has its strategic position in Southeast Asia and its industrious and resourceful population. It is now a modern island city state with the third highest per capita income in Asia after Brunei and Japan.

Singapore is not self-sufficient in food nor do its reservoirs collect enough water for the population. Instead it has to supplement its water supply from Malaysia. This water is not free and is becoming more expensive to buy. Fortunately, Singapore has a stable government and an English-speaking workforce which is one of the best educated in the region. Life in Singapore for its citizens is stressful because the people must work hard and respond and adapt quickly and effectively to drastic and rapid changes for the country to prosper and to survive.

With a total land area of only 647.5 square kilometres, the overall population density in Singapore is 4,612 persons per square kilometre (1995). In comparison, Hong Kong has an overall population density of 5,000 persons per square kilometre. Interestingly, findings in Hong Kong indicate that high-density living does not produce stress on the

Chinese adults. Certain traditional ways of living and the coping mechanism among the Chinese population may be conducive to the development of density tolerance (Ward, 1970; Anderson, 1972; Miller, 1979; Lee, 1985). In the years to come, the population density in Singapore will increase. With good planning and utilization of land and space, the ill effects of high-density living will hopefully not be as strong as they might have been.

Education is important in Singapore. Parents will endure much hardship to ensure that their young get the best education so as to guarantee them a prosperous future. The government also invests heavily in education and in the skills training of its young. Thus, the level of education attained by the young for both sexes is extremely high.

In Singapore, the young attend primary school from age 6 to 12; continue secondary education from 13 to 16; and proceed to either college or university. Boys do two and a half years of national service at 18.

In a 1995 General Household Survey, it was found that 47% of males and 41% of females in the 25–29 age group have attained polytechnic/university education. In the same survey, it was also reported that only 2.7% of the population in Singapore in the same year were found unemployed.

Patterns

Suicide under the age of 12 in any country is extremely rare. Suicide only becomes more common after 12. What are the factors which protect children from suicide? A possibility is that the child's life in a family and at school provides greater social and emotional support than that usually available in adult life. Another is that there must be a degree of cognitive maturity before a child experiences feelings such as despair and hopelessness. Other relevant cognitive abilities that develop in adolescence but are found lacking in children

Table 3.1: Young suicide rate by sex in 22 selected countries

Age group	5–14			15–24		
	Rate		'Male to female ratio'	Rate		'Male to female ratio'
Country/Sex	Male	Female		Male	Female	
Mauritus	1 (7)	4 (1)	0.3:1	17.6 (10)	13.9 (2)	1.3:1
Mexico	0.4 (20)	0.2 (15)	2:1	5.8 (19)	1.2 (21)	4.8:1
Trinidad & Tobago	0.7 (15)	2.9 (2)	0.2:1	36.8 (16)	9.7 (5)	3.8:1
Canada	1 (7)	0.5 (9)	2:1	27.7 (4)	4 (16)	7:1
USA	1.1 (7)	0.4 (6)	2:1	22 (9)	3.9 (16)	5.5:1
Denmark	1 (7)	–	–	12.6 (14)	3.4 (19)	3.7:1
Finland	0.9 (13)	0.3 (14)	3:1	35.2 (2)	8.3 (6)	4.2:1
Greece	0.6 (17)	–	–	4 (22)	0.7 (22)	5.7:1
Hungary	1.3 (4)	0.3 (14)	4.3:1	25 (8)	5.7 (11)	4.4:1
Kazakhstan	3.1 (1)	0.4 (9)	7.8:1	26.3 (6)	12.7 (3)	2.1:1
Kyrgystan	3.1 (1)	0.8 (3)	3.9:1	13.5 (13)	7.9 (7)	1.7:1
Norway	1.5 (4)	0.4 (9)	3.8:1	27.4 (5)	4.5 (18)	6.1:1
Russian Federation	2.6 (3)	0.6 (5)	4.3:1	29.5 (3)	6.6 (9)	4.5:1
Sweden	0.8 (14)	0.2 (15)	4:1	14.7 (12)	5.3 (11)	2.8:1
UK	0.1 (22)	–	–	12.2 (16)	2.3 (20)	5.3:1
Australia	0.3 (21)	0.2 (15)	1.5:1	25.6 (7)	5 (14)	5.1:1
New Zealand	1.5 (4)	–	–	38.7 (1)	5.8 (10)	6.7:1
China (selected rural)	1.1 (7)	0.7 (4)	1.4:1	16.2 (11)	35.1 (1)	0.5:1
China (selected urban)	0.5 (18)	0.4 (9)	1.3:1	6.1 (20)	10.3 (4)	0.6:1
Hong Kong	0.5 (18)	0.5 (6)	1:1	7.3 (19)	5.6 (11)	1.3:1
Singapore *	1 (7)	0.5 (6)	2:1	13.5 (14)	7.5 (8)	1.8:1
Japan	0.7 (15)	0.4 (9)	1.8:1	10.2 (17)	4.7 (15)	2.2:1

Source: World Health Statistics Annual. World Health Organization, Geneva, 1994.
*'Reports on Registration of Births and Deaths 1990'. Registry of Births and Deaths. National Registration Department, Singapore.

( ) = ranking
Rate: No of suicides per 100,000 population per annum.

include a greater awareness of self and an ability to think abstractly. Children have vague ideas about death. They often view death as a kind of sleep or a reversible journey and also they rarely see themselves as a possible agent of their own deaths (McIntyre and Angle, 1970).

It is said that only after early adolescence, around the age of 13, do children begin to grasp the concept of death as 'the end of existence' (Piaget, 1960; Koocher, 1964). Elkind (1967) described the 'personal fable', referring to adolescents' belief that they are somehow special and as a result, immune to harm.

Table 3.1 compares the suicide rates among the 5 to 14-year-olds and the 15 to 24-year-olds in Singapore with those in 21 selected countries. From the table, it can be noted that:

1. Compared to the other 21 countries, the male suicide rate among the 5 to 14-year-olds in Singapore ranked 7th and the female suicide rate ranked 6th. Compared to the other 21 countries, the male suicide rate among the 15 to 24-year-olds in Singapore ranked 14th but the female suicide rate ranked 8th.

   Interestingly, among the 15 to 24-year-olds, the female suicide rates in selected rural and urban China, Singapore and Hong Kong ranked highly – 1st, 4th, 8th and 11th respectively.

   Yap (1958) in Hong Kong, first noted that the Chinese females more than the males would kill themselves because of their low status in a patriarchal society. It was said that the traditional Chinese society did not permit their females to directly retaliate against those who aggrieved or frustrated them. Instead, the culture supported the idea of suicide as an indirect form of revenge against one who provoked them.

2. The young female suicide rates of both Mauritius and Trinidad & Tobago also ranked highly. Mauritius and Trinidad & Tobago are countries that are highly

Table 3.2: Young suicide 1-year age intervals (1969–76) in Singapore

	No		
Age/Sex	**Male**	**Female**	**Total**
7	1	–	1
10	–	1	1
11	1	–	1
12	–	1	1
13	3	1	4
14	2	2	4
15	3	8	11
16	4	12	16
17	10	19	29
18	8	15	23
19	28	18	46
All	60	77	137

Source: Chia BH. *Suicide in Singapore.* MD thesis, University of Singapore, 1978.

populated by Indians. The vulnerability of young Indian females to suicide has been reported before by several Indian researchers (Sathyavathi, 1961 and 1976; Dissanayake and Padmal De Silva, 1983).

As the rates of young suicide are low, the number of suicides in a small country like Singapore would be small. In Singapore (1969–76), there were only 2 cases of suicide in the 10 and below year-olds (table 3.2). There was 1 case of suicide each in the 11 and 12-year-olds and there were 4 cases each in the 13 and 14-year-olds. After the age of 14, the number of cases increased rapidly.

Among the 15 to 24-year-olds, suicide as a cause of death ranked 2nd for males but 1st for females in Singapore. In the United States, suicide as a cause of death ranked 2nd

(Shaffer and Fisher, 1981). Also, in Singapore, among the 15 to 24-year-olds, suicide accounted for 15%, but among the above 60-year-olds, it accounted for only 1% of total deaths (1990). Therefore, in Singapore as in other countries, suicide as a cause of death is important.

In most Western countries, young male suicides outnumber those of young female suicides by a factor of about four. Researchers from the West have said that the difference in rates between male and female might be due to biological as well as social issues.

Biologically, Hall (1978) and Schonert (1992) reported that girls, unlike boys, can better verbalize their feelings of frustration and unhappiness without acting on them. In contrast, boys are by nature more action orientated. They often cope by 'doing something about it'.

Socially, the culture's expectations for males differ from those for females. Males were traditionally 'hunters/gatherers' and females were 'caretakers'. Boys are socialized very differently from girls. They are educated from young to have different expectations of life and to develop emotionally and intellectually in different ways. In their daily lives, they are subjected to different norms of behaviour.

In some Asian societies (e.g. Islamic), females have only a domestic role and are restricted to the home and not allowed to work outside while in other societies, females play a major role in the wider economic system (Ember and Ember, 1985). In Western societies, young females have more options than young males as they grow up to adulthood. They are often not as desperate as their male peers. However, Retterstol (1993) predicted that when females become truly equal to males in the labour force and have similar expectations as males, then their suicide rates may become more like those of the males.

Rosaldo and Lampherem (1984) have suggested that the subjugation of females in their relegation to the domestic rather than the public sphere of life is a universal phenomenon common to all societies. In Asia, the females in traditional Chinese and Indian societies are particularly subjugated. Sometimes, they are so dominated by their males and not supported by their societies that they have few options but to commit suicide when humiliated and rejected.

From table 3.1, for the 15–24 age group, the male to female ratios of China (selected rural and urban), Hong Kong and Singapore (countries populated mainly by Chinese) were 0.5:1, 0.6:1 (reverse), 1.5:1 and 1.5:1 respectively. Interestingly, the male to female ratio of Thailand, another Asian country, was also reversed: 0.6:1 (Choprapawon and Visalyaputra, 1992).

From table 3.1, it can be noted that Trinidad & Tobago and Mauritius are the other countries found with reversed male to female ratios. These are countries with a high percentage of Indian populations.

Trends

Table 3.3 traces the trend of young suicides rates of 15 selected Western countries (1950–89). In 11 out of the 15 countries, the suicide rates are increasing.

The reasons quoted for the increase in Western countries are:

1. The altered of attitude of those in Western countries towards suicide: taking one's life is becoming more acceptable.
2. The strong increase in economic problems.
3. A sharp rise in youth unemployment.

Table 3.3: Trend of young suicide rate (5–24 age group) in 15 countries

Country/Year	Rate							
	50–54	55–59	60–64	65–69	70–74	75–79	80–84	85–89
Canada	2.5	2.5	3.5	5.5	10	14	15	14.5
USA	3	3	3.5	5	8	10.5	11	12
Denmark	7.5	6	6	5.5	7	7	9	9
Finland	10.5	8.5	9	10	16	21.5	19	21
France	3.5	3	3	4	5.5	7.5	8.5	8.5
Ireland	0.6	0.4	0.6	0.6	1.5	3.5	4.5	6.5
Italy	2.5	2.5	2	2	2	2.4	2.5	3
Netherlands	1.5	1.5	1.5	2	3.5	4	4	5.5
Norway	2	1.5	2	3.5	4.5	7.5	11.5	13.5
Spain	2.5	2	1.5	1	2.5	4	4.5	4
Sweden	4.5	4	6	8	9.5	9	8	9.5
Switzerland	11.5	11.5	10.5	10.5	12	16	19.5	16
UK	2	2	3	3	3	3	4	5
Australia	4	3.5	4.5	5	7	8	9.5	13
New Zealand	3.5	3	2.5	3.5	5	7	9.5	16

Source: *World Health Statistics Annual.* World Health Organization, Geneva, 1994.
Rate: No of suicides per 100,000 population per annum

4. The onset of major depressive disorder at an earlier age.
5. The increased availability of methods for suicide (Hawton, 1986).

In Australia, the suicide rates of the young are also rising. Reasons given for this rise included better recognition of young suicide by coroners (Kosky, 1987), greater availability of suicide methods (Snowden, 1989), increase in alcohol abuse (Godney and Burvill, 1989), increase in family pathology (Hassan, 1987), and increase in unemployment (Hassan and Carr, 1989).

In Hong Kong, Shek (1993) reported that the suicide rates for the young had been relatively stable for the past decade. In Taiwan, it was recorded that the peak of suicide rates observed for the young in the past has disappeared. The young in Taiwan now enjoy better material lives than their parents did and they are better safeguarded by their parents against most socioeconomic stressful situations (Chong and Cheng, 1995).

In Singapore, the proportion of young in the total population is decreasing, the education attainment by the young is high, and more importantly, the education and skills training of the young are tailored to meet the needs of the industries and employment availability (Holinger et al., 1994). The unemployment percentage of the young is low. Alcohol and drug problems for the young, unlike in the West, is relatively fewer and manageable.

However, in Singapore, both parents in the family now have to work to earn sufficient income to support the family. They have less time for their children. Very often their children are looked after by maids rather than by the parents or grandparents. Also, the young in Singapore are fast adopting the Western style of living and of coping with life problems.

Singapore, like all the other Asian countries, is currently facing one of the worst economic crises in its history. Retrenchment, unemployment, economic problems and much uncertainty are likely. Suicide rates for all age groups in these countries, including Singapore, will increase.

All these factors are important and they will affect the suicide rates of the young in Singapore in the years to come.

Chart 3.4 traces the trend of the suicide rates among the 10 to 19-year-olds in Singapore (1954 to 1997). From the chart, it can be noted that the suicide rates among the 10 to 19-year-olds in Singapore fluctuate from 1.8 to 4.2. However, in a breakdown by sex, it can be noted that the male suicide rates among the 10 to 19-year-olds appear to be increasing. This is not the case with the female suicide rates.

Chart 3.4: Trend of suicide rates among 10 to 19-year-olds in Singapore

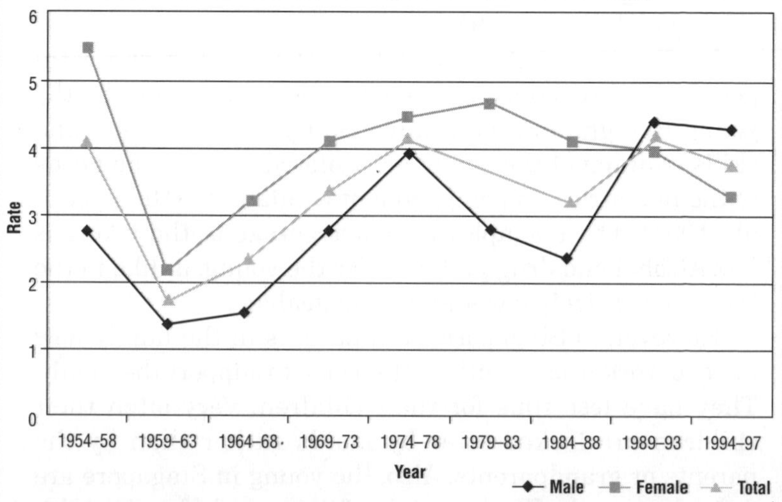

In Singapore, young males face stress in university and at work. The 'theme' for Singapore is 'excellence' for all. To achieve 'excellence', the young males must push themselves to the limits of their abilities. Status to them is very important and they will try to attain it at all cost. Failure becomes difficult to accept. Also, unlike their female counterparts, the males in Singapore have to do two and a half years of compulsory national service.

More and more young females in Singapore are receiving tertiary education, getting better paid jobs and able to stand up to their parents or husbands if unfairly treated. They, therefore, have more personal benefits such as financial independence, self-confidence, competence, self-worth and power than their predecessors. This situation is far different from days of the past when females were subjugated.

However, in Portugal, DeCastro et al. (1988) found that the gradual increase in independence of women resulted instead in a steady increase of their suicide rates in that country. Thus, the present trend that we see in Singapore may in future change.

4
Why Do the Young Commit Suicide?

In Singapore, a suicide verdict can only be given by the coroner at a coroners' inquest. At the inquest, the coroner listens to evidence from witnesses and from the police inspector in charge of the case. The medical/forensic pathologist's reports on the case and suicide letter/s (if any) are presented to the coroner. To arrive at a suicide verdict, the coroner must prove that there is suicide intent. The predisposing and precipitating factors associated with the suicide are elicited from the witnesses and recorded by the coroners in the suicide case-file.

The information given by the witnesses at the inquest and recorded in the case-files are often found to be superficial and incomplete. In my study (1978), I had to supplement these with a psychological postmortem study obtained by interviewing the parents at their homes three to six months after the suicide. At these interviews, the parents were often found to be still in shock and in distress. Thus, the recollection of the informants might have been distorted by grief, the effects of the suicide and the passage of time.

My findings are illustrated in table 4.1. However, important information, such as the individual's personality makeup and his mental state at the time of the act were often found lacking (Hawton, 1986).

Table 4.1: Predisposing and precitating factors found associated with young suicide in Singapore

Factor/Sex	Male (n=59)	Female (n=78)	Total (n=137)	
	No (%)			
Predisposing factors				
Physical illness	5 (8.5%)	4 (5%)	9 (6.5%)	
Mental illness	19 (32%)	13 (16.5%)	32 (23.5%)	x2 = 3.7, df 1, p<0.1
psychosis	13	11	24	
affective disorder	2	1	3	
personality disorder	3	1	4	
chronic drug abuse	1	–	1	
Precipitating factors				
Relationship problems	17 (29%)	39 (50%)	56 (41%)	x2= 3.11, df 1, p<0.1
dispute/being reprimanded	9	16	25	
love problems	4	10	14	
marital problems	3	9	12	
family problems	1	3	4	
bereavement	–	1	1	
Job/financial problems	5 (8.5%)	8 (10.5%)	13 (9.5%)	
Social problems	13 (22%)	14 (18%)	27 (19.5%)	
national service	11	–	11	
poor examination results	–	10	10	
having no relative	2	4	6	

Source: Chia BH. *Suicidal Behaviour in Singapore.* Tokyo: SEAMIC, 1981.

In Singapore, as shown in table 4.1, the predisposing factors found associated with young suicides were illness (mainly mental), personality disorder and chronic drug abuse. The precipitating factors found were relationship problems, job/financial problems, and social problems.

In Hong Kong, based on the perusal of 23 young suicides' records, Lo (1992) found that schizophrenia was the dominant cause of suicides in over half of the cases. The other causes found were relationship problems (family/love/marital problems, and bereavement), job/financial problems, and social problems (school/examination problems). Many of the cases of young suicides in Hong Kong came from unsatisfactory home environments.

In Western countries, 65–90% of various samples of young suicides (Shaffer, 1974; Poteet, 1987; Hoberman and Garfinkel, 1989) were reported to have experienced precipitants before their deaths. Compared with general population and controls, the significant precipitants found for the young suicides in these countries were confrontation with parents, loss of a parent, abuse or assault of girls (family pathology), disciplinary crisis in school, and conflict with the law (Carrigan et al., 1985; Kosky, 1987; Brent et al., 1988; Hoberman and Garkindel, 1988). Males appeared to be more affected by relationship breakups whereas females showed an increasing association with assault (Hagnell and Rorsman, 1980).

In Australia, legal and disciplinary problems were the stress found important in young suicides. These involved mainly criminal charges but included a few cases who were sacked from jobs or expelled from school (Graham and Burvill, 1992).

The nature of the precipitants for young suicides varies according to the social environments. A major stress in one setting might be less significant in another because of differences in culture and social expectations.

In Singapore, 70% of young suicides were precipitated by stressful life events. Many experts in Western countries also emphasize the importance of stressful life events as the cause/s of suicides in the young (Holinger et al., 1994). However, we must also realize that these stressful life events also occur in the lives of most young who do not commit suicide. Stressful life events, in themselves, probably do not pose a risk for the average young. Instead, it is the occurrence of these stressful life events in individuals with mental illness and personality disorder that create a climate of risk (Hoberman and Garkinkel, 1989).

Stressful life events

From the study of suicide letters, we can have a better understanding of how stressful life events precipitated the young in Singapore to commit suicide.

Relationship problems

Being reprimanded

A 17-year-old unemployed Chinese male. He was reprimanded by his parents for being lazy. He drowned himself. He wrote:

Why do I want to commit suicide?

It is because in the house if I am not scolded by my parents, I am scolded by my elder and younger brothers, elder and younger sisters. They ask me why I don't go to work. I was unable to think of what to do. Therefore, I just kept quiet, allowing my parents to scold me. But they keep on scolding me nonstop. Therefore, I take this course.

Now I am dead and I believe my parents will be happy about it, especially my mother who used to scold me for not going to work despite my having attained 17 or 19 years of age, but she did not scold others. When my younger brother was carrying water, my mother used to scold me and ask me why I, being older than he, do not do it instead of allowing my younger brother to do it.

But she does not know how miserable I am in my heart. At times, mother even says that those who do not work will not be allowed to eat and will have to wash their own clothes and buy their own soap. Therefore, I want to commit suicide. Now, you can all enjoy your meals heartily. Pretend to be kind. At 9 am sharp I leave never to return.

Love problems

1. A 20-year-old Chinese female secretary. She jumped from a high-rise flat. She wrote:

Dearest d ....

I trusted you and loved you so very much and I believed that you did love me too. I remember this time last you told me that you truly loved me. You promised me that you would never forsake me and would always take good care of me and you wanted me to love you always and never to leave you. You swore that that woman meant nothing to you but you felt pity for her and was only helping her. We even planned the home and life you wanted me to share with you and I was sure that you were sincere and gave up my boyfriend and many other things for I loved you true.

Your birthday card reads:

Looming ahead is sweeter knowing that there will always be new happiness for us to share.

Now my heart is so broken and there is nothing sweet for me to look ahead to. That woman got you and is sharing all the new happiness with you. It's easy for you to tell me to forget everything. It's not the end of the world. I was so humiliated when you deserted me without explanation.

Just ask yourself: Have I ever done anything against your wish? I tried to do everything for you to please you in every way and to listen to you though I did not know how to entertain you like that professional woman from 'Archinta'. You took advantage of my being weak and meek and bullied me. You hurt me more than you realized. All these months, I had been sick physically and mentally. My cough never ceased and it hurt my lungs and head. I could hardly sleep. You did not care – not a word of apology or sympathy, you just laughed at me and said 'serves you right'.

Please I do not ask for more. Just claim what is left of me for cremation as mother is away till the end of the month and nobody knows I would do this. I do not wish anybody to interfere. I have left a note telling my family not to cause you any further trouble.

Many a time you said I am educated. Do you think education can stop heartbreak and take away the horrible things you said to me? Even a good secure job, all the material things money could buy and going away to other countries meant nothing to me when you treated me so. These few months I moved around without feelings, faith, hope and trust. Nothing to look ahead to. I love you, love you eternally. I miss you so very much darling though you do not care for me now. Good-bye. My love is only for you.

2. A 17-year-old Chinese female factory worker. She drank methyl salicylate acid. She wrote:

One mistake leads to endless misery and regret.

This saying is true. This morning you asked me to leave you. I will forever remember those words. I will never forget them. Why should I be so passionate? I hate myself for having no control of myself. Because of my passion, I am in this present state of anguish. Passion leaves behind nothing but hatred. To eliminate all anguish, I have decided to die. Only death can stop this misery. Love must be mutual otherwise there will be no result. I do not want to embarrass you.

Marital problems

A 24-year-old Chinese housewife. She drank insecticide and jumped from her own high-rise flat. She wrote:

.... (husband),

I am leaving. I hope you will attend my funeral. I hate you as you have ruined my whole life. I shall not rest in peace with closed eyes. Please take care of my son. Since I got married I have not enjoyed a day of happiness. How bitter a life I have led.

In Singapore, the suicide rate for young married females was much higher than the suicide rate for young single females (Chia, 1978). Also, in Singapore, 12% of young female suicides were precipitated by marital problems (table 4.1). Thus, in Singapore, marriage did not seem to protect young females from suicide but might instead push them to suicide.

In the United Kingdom, suicides were also found to be more common among married than single young (Petzel and Cline, 1978). These young marriages were often forced by pregnancy or were hastily established as a means of escaping from an unhappy home environment and were hence likely to encounter major difficulties (Shaffer, 1974).

Family problems

A 13-year-old Chinese male student. His father was a businessman. He hanged himself. He wrote:

It is 2 am. I am in the kitchen. I am going to kill myself. It is better this way. I am depressed. I do not know why exactly. I supposed it is because of my school results. I envy my elder brother. He has got a motorcycle. He is going to Australia. Dad loves me and that's why he does not want to get me a motorcycle. Sometimes I wish he hates me a little. I have been hiding my feelings from them. I do not want them to get suspicious. How long have I been planning this? About one month.

Mother does not take much notice of me nowadays. Sister is so spoilt and she is allowed to be so rude. I guess you think I cannot be responsible. When I see a show you do not say to her, 'Brother will take you'. Instead you say, 'Sister will take you'. Instead of giving me money you give it to that stupid girl even though you know that she has got no pocket in her dress. I cannot even see a show alone. If I ask whether I can, you will start asking an awful lot of questions.

Dad is not adventurous. He always out making money. When I ask him to play chess, he will say – 'No'. Shall we go fishing? – 'No'. Let's go to Batam. – 'No'. Can I go to Kuala Lumpur? – 'No'. Not only that, you will not explain why but you just say loftily – 'I have my reasons'. If I want my own passport like all the other boys, you will demand 'What for?' or 'Why?' Can I have an air rifle – 'No'. Blah, Blah, Blah!

I wonder if there is a heaven and a hell. I wonder what it is like to feel your life ebbing. But life is cheap. Isn't it? I want to be cremated and my ashes scattered over the north and south islands of New Zealand. If you want me to come back as a ghost, I shall see what I can do. Good-bye.

The relationship between the young and their parents should be intimate and rewarding. However, tragically for some, it is alienated, hostile and destructive. In times of crisis, parents of these young could not understand their young's emotional confusion and could not help them in their moment of need. The more warmth, love and security a child can receive from his parents during the formative years of life, the better equipped he will be to cope with crises in life.

In Singapore, it has been reported that the mothers of about 7% of young suicides were mentally ill and the close relatives of 4% of young suicides had suicidal behaviour. In Western countries, Shafii et al. (1985) and Roy (1989) reported that 25–50% of young suicides had a family history of mental illness and/or suicide. The young suicides also suffered greater family pathology such as loss, neglect, and abuse and assault (Blumenthal and Kupfer, 1988).

Bereavement

1. A 19-year-old Chinese housewife. Her husband, a labourer, had recently committed suicide. She jumped from her own high rise-rise flat. She wrote:

I want to die because my husband has left me. Distribute my properties. Bury me together with my husband who had committed suicide at Selegie high-rise flat. I cannot part from him.

2. An 18-year-old Chinese female domestic worker. Her boyfriend had died in a traffic accident. She jumped from her employer's flat. She wrote:

Anything that is lost can be recovered except friendliness which is hard to retrieve. There are only feelings of disappointment and loneliness. Whether right or wrong, success or failure, it will become nothing as one turns one's head. The green mountain is there as it was, but how often is the setting sun red?

This is a very quiet evening and I am on the balcony recalling my past dream. Life is really complicated. What one encounters is quite different from what others encounter. Whatever one does creates oneself or destroys oneself. I belong to the latter.

Ruminating over that past, I find only untold misery. In the twinkling of an eye, it is the weather of spring in December. The flowers of spring bloom. Happy people are waiting for this new year to come but I am still intoxicated with darkness and greyness.

It is over a month since you left. There is not a day in this month that I did not think of you. I used to call your name softly, hoping that you will rush towards me. But on scrutinizing the shadow which flies past there is just a picture of nothingness. Now you rest forever. You sleep quietly forever. However, I can no more recall your response. I cannot see your smile. I cannot get your kiss anymore. On the evening when we were betrothed beside the fresh water-pool the feeling between us had been good.

As a human there is always hope. The beautiful dream has now changed into emptiness. The pledge between us two has now changed into bubbles. I have already lost a heart – you.

Social problems

In Singapore, the main social precipitant found for young male suicides was national service and for female suicides, it was poor examination results.

National service

A 21-year-old Chinese male serving national service. He jumped from a high-rise flat. He could not cope with life in the army. He became paranoid and depressed. He wrote:

Please forgive me. Buy me the cheapest coffin and burn my dead body. I love you all and make you all suffer. Good-bye.

Examination problems

A 18-year-old Chinese female student. She was worried about the outcome of her school examinations results and became depressed. She jumped from her high-rise flat. She wrote:

I am in such a state of mental agony. I have tried very hard to make progress in my studies. However, during the examination period, I could not sleep. These sufferings have been most unbearable. My mental health is on the brink of collapse. What shall I do?

I have disappointed you before by failing my exams, but there won't be any third time. I am the black sheep of this family, a good for nothing. It is useless for me to be here. I have enough of this dull and miserable life. Enough of humiliation from my family.

Ever since I've failed my exams, I could not bring myself to study again. I stopped attending classes. I hate to continue on after trying so hard for the exams and yet failing. Mother, I can't repay you for what you have done for me but I will do so in the next world.

Job and financial problems

Job/financial problems were the precipitants found for 9.5% of the total young suicides in Singapore.

Job problems

A 20-year-old Chinese female park attendant. She jumped from a high-rise flat. She wrote:

Today, at the company, we lost $5. The person who was working with me told the supervisor again and again that never before had the company lost so much money and that she did not want to work anymore. What is that supposed to mean? She must imply that it was the new chap (me) who took the money. To die is the only way to prove my innocence. I am the new chap and cannot give the company an explanation. I am sure she was the guilty one.

She even taught me that if any money was missing we could first repay the company but later we could take it back from the company and no one would know about it. Once, when I was working with her, $1 was missing. She repaid it this morning but later took it back from the company and asked me not to tell the other colleagues. Thus, I am sure she is the culprit.

I hope she will realize that there is someone who is willing to do something foolish in spite of her innocence so that the guilty one will make a confession to the company. I shall not let her go so easily. I shall forever follow her because she has made me suffer. I hope that the company will make a thorough investigation into this matter.

Ilness and personality disorder

Mental illness and personality disorder are important factors found associated with young suicide. In Western countries, evidence from numerous psychological postmortem studies of young suicide have indicated that over 90% of those who committed suicide suffered symptoms meeting the diagnostic criterion of these two conditions (Shaffer, 1988). In the Asian countries, the percentages found were much lower but this is most probably due to under-diagnosis.

For the young suicides in Singapore, Chia (1978) found only 30% suffered from illness (mainly mental illness). This is much lower compared with those found in Western countries.

Physical illness

In Singapore, only 7% of young suicides were found associated with physical illness (table 4.1). Cosand et al. (1982) in the United States and Hawton (1986) in the United Kingdom also reported that physical illness rarely appeared to be a major contributing factor in adolescent and child suicides.

A cardiac cripple

A 19-year-old unemployed Chinese male. His mother was a washerwoman. He was a cardiac cripple. He jumped from a high-rise flat. He wrote:

Time passes by very swiftly. Time flows away like water of the flowing stream. Time passes away one year after another. Spring has come again. How is it that I have to lead such a bitter life while you all lead such interesting lives? It seems that I have to live in anguish throughout my lifetime. I must view my world as unchangeable.

Why must I live a life drained of spirit and love? Every day and night at the hospital window side I cast my thoughts over this agonizing situation. It is like a silent dream. While pondering, tears will roll down my eyes like raindrops falling from the sky. My thoughts are like dark clouds over the blue sky.

Mental illness

In Singapore, about 23% of young suicides were found associated with mental illness (more males than females). In Hong Kong, Lo (1992) found that over half of young suicides (10–24) were found to be mentally ill, mostly from schizophrenia. In the West, Shaffer et al. (1988) have asserted that 'mental illness is a necessary condition for suicide'. Most young who kill themselves meet the criteria for diagnosable psychiatric disorders (Blumenthal and Kupfer, 1988; Shaffer et al., 1985).

In a diagnostic breakdown of young suicides in Singapore, as shown in table 4.1, about 18% of the young suicides were found associated with psychosis (mainly schizophrenia) but only about 2% were found associated with affective disorder.

Schizophrenia

A 13-year-old Chinese male student. His father was a Chinese physician. He drank corrosive. He wrote:

Please pardon me for not being filial. I have not been able to overcome the 'psychological contradiction' within me which pushes me to commit suicide. Truthfully, I do not know why I want to die. My 'mind' persistently drives me to act thus.

Today, at my medical checkup, the doctor advised me to consult a psychiatrist as soon as possible. Most shocking indeed! Most outrageous! Someone points at you and tells you that you are 'mentally deranged'. No! I am not deranged. The one who is mentally deranged is the doctor.

In the Western countries, affective disorder has been found in approximately 25–75% of young suicides (Carrigan et al., 1985). Therefore, in comparison, the percentage of young suicides in Singapore found associated with affective disorder was low. However, as said before, this is probably due to under-diagnosis.

In Singapore, about 30% of young suicide letter-writers expressed feelings of anguish/despair/depression but about 18% expressed feelings of anger/hate. It can also be noted that a signficantly higher percentage of young compared to old suicide letter-writers expressed these negative feelings (table 6.1).

In Western countries, Brent et al.(1988) and Hoberman and Garkindel (1989) also found anger in 25–33% of their depressed subjects. Toolan (1975) also reported that unlike old suicides, young suicides were more often associated with anger.

Studies on affective disorder among the ethnic Chinese have revealed that they would more often express their emotions in physical rather than psychological symptoms (Ots, 1990). Therefore, the diagnosis of affective disorder can be missed because of the facade of somatic symptoms (Lau et al., 1983).

Chinese parents, especially mothers, demonstrate love and care through expressing concern over and taking care of their children's bodily functions and needs. It has been said that a Chinese child who complains of abdominal cramps will be given warm soup to eat and tenderly cared for while a child who expresses fear will possibly be scolded. Thus, overt expression of affection is discouraged. Somatized presentation and behaviour is sanctioned and nurtured leading to somatic preoccupation.

The verbal expression of emotion in the Chinese language is predominantly somatic orientated. The closest expression of a state of depression in the Chinese language is *sing ging bu hou* (the condition of my heart is not good), a somatic description (Hsu, 1985). In Taiwan, in the two languages (Hokkien and Mandarin) spoken on the island, there is an impoverishment of words referring to psychological states, and often words meaning 'troubled' or 'anxious' are expressed in terms of bodily organs (Kleinman, 1989).

In the nosology of traditional Chinese medicine, 'liver' is a metaphor for anger, 'heart' for anxiety and 'spleen' for depression. To traditional Chinese practitioners, emotions are pathogenic factors which cause disturbance of the organs and their functions. Treatment would therefore not consist of psychotherapy but aim instead at harmonizing the bodily functions by herbal medicines or acupuncture.

The Chinese are also reserved in expressing their feelings, avoiding the open display of emotions which may reveal weakness and disrupt social harmony or convey the stigma of mental illness.

In a study of cases of depression presented to a private general practice in Hong Kong, it was found that 96% of the sample had initially complained of somatic symptoms. Practically no depressed patient initially mentioned emotional distress as the chief complaint. Eighty five per cent in all had 'aches and pains' of some description. Headaches were present in 85% of the sample. The other somatic complaints were epigastric discomfort, dizziness, general malaise, feverishness, cough, menstrual disturbances and low back pain (Lau et al., 1983).

In my own practice, I find many patients, especially those less educated and older, will not accept depressive disorder as a disease entity.

However, somatization was not exclusive to Chinese patients but was also commonly found in other non-Western countries and among lower social classes and less well-educated patients in Western countries (Singer, 1975).

In Singapore, young Chinese suicides in their letters sometimes expressed their feelings of untold grievances, anger, grief, remorse and despair in a 'romantic Chinese way'.

Examples from suicide letters

1. I stood at the window side pondering and tears will roll down my eyes like raindrops falling from the sky. The thoughts in my mind are like dark clouds floating over the sky.

2. Who knows of my present mood? Shedding tears on my pillow until dawn just like the raindrops falling on the doorsteps. Drops of tears. Love. Broken heart. Broken and in grief.
3. Silkworms of springtime will not exhaust yielding silk until the time of their death. Tears will not dry up until the burning candle has burned into ashes.
4. The tree wants to be at rest but the breeze will not cease blowing.
5. I felt my heart being stabbed by a thousand knives. I will be in anguish for the rest of my life.

Interestingly, the Japanese also do not experience depression in the same way Westerners do nor do they express their feelings as Westerners do. For the Japanese, concrete images from nature allow personal emotions to be expressed impersonally (Tanaka-Matshmi and Marsella, 1976).

Diagnosis of affective disorder in the young is not easy. In Western countries, studies have demonstrated that neither parents nor teachers are accurate judges of depression in children or adolescents. Consequently, studies of young suicide based on information from them are likely to under-diagnose the percentage of them found suffering from affective disorder (Lefkowitz and Tesiny, 1980; Sacco and Graves, 1986). Toolan (1975) reported that depression was 'often masked by acting-out tendencies' in younger people.

Also, in Western countries, Calson and Cantwell (1982) found that the relationship between depressive disorder and suicidality is complex. It should be emphasized that most depressed young are not suicidal. Shaffer and Bacon (1989) estimated the risk ratio of depressed to depressed suicidal adolescents as 660:1. However, table 4.2 shows that the risk ratio for the depressed Chinese patients treated in a private psychiatric clinic in Singapore was 52:1.

Table 4.2: Diagnosis and follow-up finding of young patients treated in a private psychiatric clinic in Singapore

	No (%)		
Diagnosis	Patients treated (P)	Patients who had committed suicide (S)	Risk ratio (P:S)
Schizophrenia	417	15	28:1
Organic psychosis	26	–	–
Paranoid disorder	44	1	44:1
Affective disorder	362	7	52:1
Neurosis	260	2	130:1
Other	166	–	–
Total	1275	25	51:1

Types of mental illness

The diagnostic breakdown of 1,275 young patients who had sought treatment in a private psychiatric clinic in Singapore is summarized in table 4.2. In a follow-up study done of these patients, it was found that 25 had committed suicide.

1. 15 suicides (60%) were diagnosed as suffering from psychosis (mainly schizophrenia).
2. 4 suicides (16%) were diagnosed as suffering from major depressive disorder, 2 suicides (8%) from manic-depressive disorder and 1 suicide (4%) from minor depressive disorder.

3. Interestingly, 2 suicides (8%) were diagnosed as suffering from panic disorder and 1 (4%) from paranoid disorder.

From table 4.2, it can be noted that the risk ratios for these patients varied from 28:1 to 130:1 depending on the diagnostic category.

In terms of number and risk ratio, schizophrenia is the most important mental illness found associated with young suicides in Singapore. When the demographic and clinical variables of 'living schizophrenic' (402 cases) and 'suicide schizophrenic' (15 cases) were compared, significant differences were found in the following variables – being unemployed, being married/separated, presence of recent stressful life events, being depressed, past history of suicidal attempt/s and relapsing illness. In Western countries, Roy (1986) found that significantly more of schizophrenic suicides than 'control' were young, male, unemployed, had in the past been diagnosed as suffering from depressive episodes and had illnesses which were chronic and relapsing.

Drake et al. (1984) have hypothesized that schizophrenic patients killed themselves because they had high performance expectations and were unable to accept the declining functional ability that schizophrenia might have caused them. Among the patients treated in a private clinic in Singapore, there were two such cases.

Schizophrenia

A 21-year-old Chinese female. She came from a respectable and happy family. She was a student in the polytechnic but failed in her recent examinations.

She felt that people had made her a subject of a 'study'. The data from the 'study' would be channelled to the mass media. Her house was bugged. She felt very upset and wanted to disappear from the face of this world. When examined, she was found to be incongruous in mood and depressed. She was reluctant to see the doctor and was non-compliant to treatment given. She also had a history of suicide attempts.

Because of her illness, she could no longer pursue her studies. She became very envious of her siblings' academic successes. She could not accept her illness and her academic failures. She jumped from a high-rise building.

Also, two suicides had auditory hallucinations instructing them to kill themselves. Two suicides had persistent paranoid delusions. One patient, unable to tolerate the severe side effect (akathisia) of antipsychotic drugs given to treat the psychosis, killed herself (Shear et al., 1983).

What is schizophrenia?

Schizophrenia is a severe psychiatric disorder. The illness usually starts in adolescence or in early adult life and often becomes chronic and disabling.

It is a complex illness characterized mainly by hallucinations (hearing voices), delusions, abnormal and aggressive behaviour, withdrawal, and disrupted social functioning.

The burden on the family is heavy and both the patient and his relatives are often exposed to stigma associated with the illness.

Antipsychotics are the cornerstone of treatment of this illness. Relapses do occur. In management, families have to be counselled and supported. Often patients have to be rehabilitated before they can return to more productive roles in the society.

For patients suffering from affective disorder, the risk ratio was 52:1. However, in a further diagnostic breakdown of affective disorder, manic-depressive disorder was the diagnostic category found with the highest suicide risk with a risk ratio of 8:1 followed by major depressive disorder with a risk ratio of 32:1.

Affective disorder

1. A 24-year-old Chinese male diagnosed as suffering from manic-depressive disorder. He jumped from his own high-rise flat. He wrote:

Concentration is bad. I worry excessively. I am tired. I have no desire to go out. I feel uncomfortable. I have to rest. I am always tense. I lose my temper easily. Fear. My chest feels 'stuffy'. I am miserable most of the time. I have no confidence that I will be cured. I despise myself intensely. Please help me to drive away these suicidal thoughts. I have no friends. I am very lonely. Frankly, I think of giving up. I am afraid of the future.

2. A 20-year-old Chinese female diagnosed as suffering from major depressive disorder. She drank detergent. She wrote:

I have sinned grievously. Because of my sins, human beings on earth have to suffer. Soon there would be no day or night on earth. Human beings will no longer be able to make a living on earth. I have to die to save mankind from this catastrophe.

Suicide might be seen by a depressed patient as a kind of absolution e.g. the painful guilt or wrong can only be cancelled by the sacrifice of a life.

What is depressive disorder?

Depressive disorder is common, often missed, not difficult to diagnose, can be severe, often recurrent and highly treatable. The symptoms found in depressive disorder are depressive mood, loss of pleasure or interest, insomnia, agitation/retardation, fatigue, increased sense of worthlessness, decreased concentration and suicide ideas.

Treatment consists of antidepressant medications, psychotherapy, cognitive therapy, electro-convulsive therapy or some combination of these treatments. With treatment, 80–90% of people with major depressive disorder will recover.

The other diagnostic categories of importance with regard to suicide risk among patients treated in a private psychiatric clinic in Singapore were paranoid disorder and neurosis (panic disorder) with risk ratios of 44:1 and 130:1 respectively.

Paranoid disorder

A 23-year-old Chinese male school teacher. He was diagnosed as suffering from paranoid disorder. He jumped from a high-rise flat. He wrote:

These last few days, I have been very depressed and worried. For reasons unknown to me, my colleagues in school have boycotted me.

Probably they misunderstood me and suspected that I was a spy. This 'boycott movement' was organized by the principal, the ringleader and two other colleagues. They plan to assault and kill me. I do not know whether the mishap will materialize. Should it happen the police should look into it and questioned the above named ....

What is paranoid disorder?

Paranoid disorder refers to a variety of conditions characterized by delusion and related behaviour that can be aggressive and dangerous.

Delusion can be defined as a false belief which is held with unusual conviction and is not amenable to logic. However, others easily recognize it as not in keeping with the person's educational and cultural background.

Delusions found in paranoid disorder are mainly persecutory, grandiose, jealous or religious in nature.

Panic disorder

An 18-year-old Chinese male first consulted a general practitioner for examination phobia. His mother, a washerwoman, described him as a timid, nervous and kindly person. His father died when he was young. He had no siblings.

Encouraged by a friend, he then visited a brothel and developed penile discharge. Thereafter he became more apprehensive and depressed. He had recurrent panic attacks. He experimented with marijuana.

In spite of treatment, he remained mentally unwell. He could not travel by bus, and at home, he was afarid to be alone. He remained unemployed and had to depend economically on his mother.

He complained bitterly that he was not leading a normal life and that he was a burden to his mother. He hanged himself.

What is panic disorder?

Panic disorder is a minor mental illness. Many patients suffering from panic disorder have their first panic attack in adolescence. However, most have their fully developed syndrome by the age of 30.

A panic attack is characterized by the rapid onset of fear, terror or discomfort accompanied by some of the following symptoms – palpitations, chest pressure, nausea, light-headedness, numbness, hot flashes or chills.

People with panic disorder have recurrent, unexpected panic attacks, often more than one attack per week. The attacks are often accompanied by one month or more of persistent concern about having additional attacks, worry about the significance of the attack or significant changes in behaviour.

Such patients become phobic and begin to avoid situations from which escape may be difficult or in which they cannot rapidly obtain help with panic symptoms. In its most severe forms, the patient is confined to his home.

Panic disorder can be treated with medication alone, cognitive behavioural treatment alone, or a combination of the two modalities.

Alcohol and drug abuse

Studies on Asian suicides have revealed that alcoholism is seldom considered the direct reason for suicide among people in Asia (Kok and Tseng, 1992). In Singapore (1969–76), there was no case of young suicide found associated with chronic alcohol abuse.

Among the three ethnic groups in Singapore, a higher percentage of young Malays smoke marijuana. In Singapore (1969–76), there was only one case (0.7%) of young suicide who chronically abused illegal drugs and he was a Malay.

Drug addiction

A young Malay male had been smoking marijuana for a long time. He was found at times 'confused'. On a few occasions he was found sleeping in the toilet. He was dismissed from his job because of poor job performance.

Thereafter he became depressed. He could not sleep at night. One day he was found dead at the foot of a block of high-rise flats.

High percentages, 33–70%, of young suicides in Western countries, however, had abused alcohol or drug (Schuckit and Schuckit, 1989).

Personality disorder

In Western countries, personality disorders (especially borderline) have been found in 25–40% of young suicides (Shaffer et al., 1985; Blumenthal and Kupfer, 1988). Hoberman and Garkindel (1988) suggested heterogeneity of personality characteristics among the young who committed suicide. Their most common categories were the 'withdrawn, lonely, supersensitive and angry'.

In Singapore, only 3% of the young suicides in Singapore were identified as suffering from personality disorder (table 4.1). Again, as in affective disorder, I feel that this percentage is probably markedly underestimated because of under-diagnosis.

Borderline personality

The deceased was a young, single, female trainee fashion designer. Her father was a clerk and her mother was a housewife. She had five siblings. They all lived in a two-room HDB flat.

When first seen, her main complaints were an inability to relate well to people, an obsession with male genital organs and an inability to relate to the opposite sex. According to her parents, she has always been a sensitive and difficult person. She was extravagant and liked to buy expensive clothes.

At work, she felt that her colleagues were criticising and humiliating her. At home, she said that she was often reprimanded by her mother.

In spite of prolonged follow-up and therapy, she remained unwell. When seen, she was often found frustrated, agitated and depressed. She had strong suicidal ideas and a feeling of hopelessness. She jumped from her high-rise flat.

Antisocial personality

The deceased was a 24-year-old male Indian Muslim. He had only completed secondary one.

The father, 50, was a daily rated overseer. The mother was a domestic helper. Two unmarried sisters, aged 17 and 18, were not working. The family was happy and not in financial trouble.

The deceased stayed with his uncle and aunt but went home to his parents occasionally. His father described him was as 'a notorious man' – a professional liar, swindler and troublemaker who had brought much shame and disgrace to the family. He was intelligent and capable of hard work but used his intelligence and ability foolishly.

Physically, he was healthy.

He ill-treated his sisters, but they still liked him and spoilt him as he was their only brother. From young he was spoilt by his mother. She would cover his faults and condone his many mistakes. At school, he gambled. The father was convinced that his son was incorrigible and often punished him.

He was extravagant – buying expensive shirts and trousers, going to film-shows, and had a habit of 'showing off'. He obtained his money by deceit – borrowing from relatives and friends, stealing his sisters' savings and pawning their jewellery. He even went so far as to tell relatives that his mother was dead in order to obtain money from them. He cheated his uncle of $2,000 by convincing the uncle that he could get him a HDB flat. He also frequently indulged in alcohol and marijuana.

Once, he worked as a warden but failed to report for work for a whole month. He wanted to resign but the officer-in-charge insisted on one month's notice. He ignored this requirement and disappeared with the uniforms and warrant card. He was imprisoned for 18 months. On discharge from prison, he worked first as a labourer and then later at a furniture shop. At both places of work he ran away with his employers' money.

Prior to his suicide, he had a girlfriend and wanted to marry her. The girl's father objected to the marriage. Thereafter, he appeared to have 'changed'. He would return home frequently to talk to his father. He wanted to save money and became concerned about his sisters' futures and marriages. The father, however, found it difficult to believe in or to trust him as the father was convinced that he was a professional liar.

He committed suicide by jumping blindfolded from a high-rise flat. In his suicide note he wrote that he was unhappy with what he had done in the past. He had ended his life because no one loved him anymore and he had been cheated in love by his girlfriend.

The father said that to commit suicide was a great sin in their religion. Thus, as a father, he was ashamed that his son had committed suicide. He was angry and sad and he blamed his wife for spoiling the deceased. However, on second thoughts, he said that the suicide was perhaps a blessing as his son, if alive, would continue to bring more shame and disgrace to the family and this would jeopardize the chances of his two younger daughters in getting married.

What is personality disorder?

Personality disorder is distinguished by chronically inadequate adaptive capacities affecting several areas of functioning such as social relationship or occupational performances. The DSM-IV subdivided personality disorders into 3 clusters:

Cluster A	odd/eccentric	paranoid, schizoid, schizotypal
Cluster B	dramatic/erratic	antisocial, borderline, histrionic
Cluster C	anxious/fearful	avoidant, dependant, obsessive-compulsive

In the United States, standardized and structured diagnostic interviews estimated the life-time prevalence of personality disorder in the general population at 10–13%.

Yeh et al. (1995) in a epidemiological study of the community population in Taiwan, found that antisocial personality and pathological gambling were the types of personality disorders found prevalent among the Chinese in Taiwan.

Sexual problems

In the West, Remafedi et al. (1991) reported that gender identity issue including homosexuality was a risk factor for young suicide. In Singapore (1969–76), there was only one case of young suicide with gender identity problem.

Transsexualism

A 19-year-old Chinese male in national service. He jumped from a high-rise flat. He was diagnosed as suffering from transsexualism.

My friend (boyfriend),

How are you? This is the third letter I'm writing this letter to you. But unlike the other two, I am shedding tears while writing this letter. It can be taken for granted that we do not have the affinity to be friends.

Hope that we can be together in the next world.

Though I depart from this world, my heart is still in love with you forever. Let me speak the truth to you. I am a 'sex man' (hermaphrodite). I realize that it is not possible for me to get married to you. So I have no alternative but to take this path. Finally, I hope that you will be able to find a pretty maiden. Wishing you handsome forever and in good physical health forever.

5

Suicide Among the Different Ethnic Groups

The Chinese

In the early history of China, many Chinese immigrated to the various parts of the world because of political and economic reasons (Tsu, 1966). In Southeast Asia, Chinese are found in Singapore, Malaysia, Thailand, Indonesia, Indochina and the Philippines. However, it is only in Singapore that the Chinese are in the majority and where they are in control politically and economically.

Singapore has a population of about 3 million (1995). The population is multi-racial, comprising 79% Chinese, 14% Malays, 6% Indians and 1% other ethnic groups.

The beliefs and way of life of the overseas Chinese are still strongly influenced by the teachings of Confucianism, Buddhism and Taoism and are very different from those of the other ethnic groups. Of importance to the Chinese are filial piety, loyalty to family, honour, revenge, education and superstitious beliefs such as yuan, fengshui and the practice of homonym (Rin, 1975). Also, the Chinese highly value material success. It is said that 'with money one is a dragon; without it, a worm' and 'men die for wealth; birds for food'.

In ancient China, traditionally, suicide was used by the Chinese as a means to show loyalty – to nation, emperor or master, wife to her dead husband, or in politics and war (Lee, 1995).

Current studies of Chinese suicide are based on the Chinese population living in Hong Kong (Yap, 1958; Lo and Leung, 1985; Lo, 1985 and 1992), Singapore (Hassan and Tan, 1970; Chia and Tsoi, 1972; Chia, 1978; Kua and Tsoi, 1985) and Taiwan (Chong et al., 1992; Chong and Cheng, 1995). A recent study of suicide in mainland China (Mingzhao et al., 1992) is also available.

Table 5.1: Comparison of young suicide rate by sex in Asian countries

Country	5–14			15–24		
	Rate		'Male to female ratio'	Rate		'Male to female ratio'
	Male	Female		Male	Female	
China (selected rural)	1 (1)	0.7 (1)	1.5:1	16 (2)	35 (1)	0.5:1
China (selected urban)	0.5 (5)	0.4 (5)	1.5:1	6 (6)	10.5 (2)	0.5:1
Hong Kong	0.5 (5)	0.5 (4)	1:1	7.5 (5)	5.5 (4)	1.5:1
Singapore (Chinese) *	0.6 (4)	0.7 (1)	0.9:1	17 (1)	7 (3)	2.5:1
Japan	0.7 (2)	0.4 (5)	2:1	10 (4)	4.5 (6)	2:1
South Korea	0.7 (2)	0.6 (3)	1.2:1	10.8 (3)	5.3 (5)	2:1

Source: *World Health Statistics Annual.* World Health Organization, Geneva, 1994.
*Report on Registration of Births and Deaths 1990. Registry of Births and Deaths. National Registration Department, Singapore.
( ) ranking.

Rate: No of suicides per 100,000 population per annum.

Patterns

Table 5.1 compares the male and female suicide rates among the 5 to 14-year-olds and 15 to 24-year-olds of Singapore with those of four other Asian countries.

Among the 10 to 14-year-olds, the male Chinese suicide rate in Singapore ranked 4th but the female Chinese rate in Singapore ranked 1st. However, among the 15 to 24-year-olds, the male Chinese suicide rate in Singapore ranked 1st and the Chinese female suicide rate ranked 3rd.

For the 5–14 age group, the mean male to female ratio of mainland China, Hong Kong and Singapore was 1.5:1. For the same age group, the mean male to female ratio of the Western countries was 3.5:1 (table 3.1). For the 15–24 age group, the mean male to female ratio of countries with a high Chinese population was 1:1 compared to 4.5:1 for the Western countries. Thus, the mean male to female ratio of young Chinese suicides differed markedly from the mean male to female ratio of young suicides in Western countries.

Yap (1958) was the first to note that the young Chinese females (Hong Kong) had much higher suicide rates than the young Chinese males. Among the 16 to 20-year-olds, the male to female ratio for Hong Kong from 1953–54 was 0.2:1. However, in 1990, among the 15 to 24-year-olds, the male to female ratio for Hong Kong was 1.5:1.

In Singapore, among the 10 to 19-year-olds, the male to female ratio from 1954–89 was 0.5:1 but from 1994–97, it was 1.3:1 (table 3.4). As in Hong Kong, there is a marked change in the male to female ratio from the past to the present in Singapore.

Young Chinese females in modern Singapore, unlike their predecessors, are now better educated, working, and financially independent of their male partners. These may be the important factors that now protect the young Chinese females in Singapore from committing suicide.

Why do young Chinese in Singapore commit suicide?

In Singapore, 61% of young Chinese suicide letter-writers gave reasons for their suicides (table 5.2). The main reasons given were relationship problems (family/love/marital problems), job/financial problems, social problems (examination problems) and illness.

Family problems

A 18-year-old Chinese female student. She drowned herself. She wrote:

Dear Daddy,

I am committing suicide. I cannot bear to stay in the house anymore. Actually for a long time I wanted to commit suicide. If I should fail and not die and become paralyzed, you would beat me.

I am a coward. I am afraid to die but it is for the better. I want to die because I cannot bear your shouting anymore. I am always so afraid of you. Whenever you shouted at mother I would tremble with fear. I knew that you could turn on me at any moment.

I know that I am not a good daughter and so if I die you will not lose anything. I know that I am full of self-pity. Even if you were to improve in your temper I shall still want to die because I know that the situation will not really change.

The traditional Chinese family organizes itself in a hierachial way. The father plays an authoritarian role. Communication usually means parents questioning and lecturing the child. The child is seldom allowed to communicate his opinions or feelings freely to the parents. Also, parents usually respond to the child's misbehaviour with criticism rather than understanding and empathy. Thus, a Chinese child generally avoids telling his parents his emotional problems. There is a lack of closeness between the child and the parents in Chinese families (Hsu, 1985).

Table 5.2: Comparison of content of suicide letters by ethnic group

Content/ethnic group	Chinese (n=75)	Indian (n=7)	Malay (n=4)
	No (%) of total suicide letters		
Reason for suicide	**46 (61.5%)**	**2 (28.5%)**	**1 (25%)**
relationship problems	25 (33.5%)	2 (28.5%)	1 (25%)
job/financial problems	15 (20%)	–	–
illness	12 (16%)	–	–
social problems	5 (6.5%)	–	–
Emotion	**42 (56%)**	**5 (71.5%)**	**2 (50%)**
gratitude	4 (5.5%)	1 (14.5%)	–
anguish/depressed	31 (41.5%)	–	1 (25%)
anger/hate	13 (17.5%)	2 (28.5%)	1 (25%)
revenge	4 (5.5%)	–	–
Instruction	**33 (44%)**	**4 (57%)**	**2 (50%)**
concern for survivor/allay	22 (29.5%)	4 (57%)	2 (50%)
corpse	14 (18.5%)	1 (14.5%)	–
possession/will	10 (13.5%)	4 (57%)	1 (25%)
Ask forgiveness	**23 (30.5%)**	**3 (43%)**	**2 (50%)**
not filial	16 (21.5%)	–	–
repay	3 (4%)	–	–
Farewell	**23 (30.5%)**	**4 (57%)**	**1 (25%)**
Exculpate	**5 (6.5%)**	**2 (28.5%)**	**–**

Love problems

A 22-year-old Chinese female clerk. She drank arsenic. She wrote:

Can you really help me if I were to tell you that I am having an affair with a married man?

He tells me that he loves me and wants me to be his second wife. You see, I am a very lonely woman. I have made a mistake of telling him of my problems concerning my first affair. He knows that I am a weak character and that I am highly 'sexed'. He takes advantage of me and he is making use of me. I did try not to see him but the moment he rang I could not say no to him.

Lately he borrowed money from me. I did tell him that I am not a very rich woman and that I am a spendthrift. When I told him that I have to support my mother he asked me to change the subject. He lies about paying for my policy. He asks gifts from me. He takes my money. He tells me that he loves me whenever he wants something from me. Lately, he does not respond to my kisses. Is he sick of me? He is selfish. He tells lies. I want to stop seeing him because I know that he is making use of me and my money.

Financial problems

A 24-year-old Chinese male businessman. He gambled and lost $35,000 of his mother's money. He jumped from his high-rise flat. He wrote:

Mother,

Your not filial son is going to part from you forever. Forgive me for spending your money. It has nothing to do with other people. Until the time of my death, I still do not know how I have spent all the money. Please treat my wife and the two kids well. Do not bear a grudge against them for they do not know what I have done. I shall repay your kindness in bringing me up in our reincarnation.

Your not filial son

Education, being the key to economic advancement, has always been important to the Chinese. Chinese parents will not spare anything to give their children a proper education. In China in the past, examinations were open to all with talent, whether rich or poor. The examinations system gave China a succession of wise and learned ministers, governors, magistrates and officials. Interestingly, in Singapore, more Chinese female than male suicides were found preceded by poor examination results.

In Hong Kong, Chinese parents also place a great emphasis on schooling and this enthusiasm has led to the great intensity of academic competition and examination pressure in the school, from kindergarten to the university (Tu, 1981). To the Hong Kongers, education is not only a means to economic gain but also has its moral value. It has been said that 'study is superior to all other walks of life'. 'Good education leads to official position' and 'golden houses and beautiful wives come through study' (Lee, 1985).

Examination problems

A 22-year-old Chinese female student. She was worried over her pending examinations result. She drank salicylate acid. She wrote:

One who is successful in life is a dragon. One who fails in life is a worm. Time flows eastwards like a stream. It flows swiftly, more doggedly and more ruthlessly than the roaring waves of the Yangtze and Hwang Ho rivers.

In Singapore, a high percentage of young Chinese committed suicide because of severe mental illness such as schizophrenia and depressive disorder.

Schizophrenia

A 24-year-old Chinese male. His business was unsuccessful and he began to drink alcohol excessively. He jumped from his high-rise flat. He wrote:

Since childhood, I have been suffering from schizophrenia. All along, I realized it. However, recently my illness has gone worse.

I am now unable to control my emotions. At times, I fear living more than dying. If I were to continue living in this condition, I cannot imagine what would happen to me in the future. When I used my brain, I often find that my mind was numbed.

I know that I am abnormal psychologically. However, my social values and moral concepts are still correct and intact. In a bus, cinema or a crowd, people stare strangely at me. Girls avoid me. How then can I feel easy at heart? To feel comfort, I therefore avoid people. I am also always arguing with my own thoughts. I want to get well soon. All along, I have not been able to give happiness. I myself know that I have no future. It has nothing to do with others. Schizophrenia breaks the heart, causes cerebral abnormality and ruins life and causes death.

Psychotic depression

A 23-year-old Chinese female seamstress. She was diagnosed as suffering from psychotic depressive disorder and had previously been admitted to a psychiatric hospital for treatment. She jumped from her high-rise flat. She wrote:

I shall have no more privilege to address you as an elder brother soon. I see that your concern for me will end this evening. I am now no better than a dog. Every minute I try to ruin myself. Did you remember what I have said.

Please select for me one other alternative. Get me admitted to Woodbridge Hospital or let me commit suicide.

At this moment I cannot cry because I have already lost the nature of being a human being. Give me the courage to die. Even if you were to save me it would be useless. I will destroy myself again in the next three months.

I have been most unfilial, unkind, cruel, vicious and sinful person. I am not a human being but an animal. Not even better than an animal. Save my soul. Pardon me papa. Oh God, pardon me. Save me.

Suicide letters

Unlike the young of other ethnic groups in Singapore, young Chinese suicides were still concerned about their corpses after their death. Instructions were left behind in their letters on how to dispose of them. Confucius had taught that one should not injure one's own body (not even one's hair and skin) because these were given to one by one's parents.

No post-mortem

A 21-year-old Chinese male private in the army. He took corrosive. He wrote:

My last wish: No operation to be performed on my body after my death. I came to this world in this condition. I would like to go back in a similar condition with no stitches in my abdomen or with an empty inside.

Twenty one per cent of young suicide letter-writers said that they had not been filial and 4% said that they would repay their parents in the next life.

In Singapore, revenge suicide was also popular among the Chinese young (5%). Revenge suicide is a common theme in Chinese stories and plays.

Revenge

A 20-year-old Chinese female secretary. She jumped from her high-rise flat. She wrote:

This damned greatest rascal has cheated me of my affection and swindled me of my money. Right from the beginning, I had told him not to come but he stubbornly kept bothering me, saying that there is no affection between him and his wife. He but feels responsible for her and what not.

Now his wife threatens to commit suicide. He telephones me to say let all bygones be bygones. Now, I realize that he is a hypocrite who goes around deceiving girls. Having acquired everything from me, he now wants to shirk from his responsibility. He thinks that he can hoodwink his friends and members of the public.

I, hereby, give warning in this letter to all young maidens not to be taken in by his trick. He is the proprietor of .... Tel. No. .... Does he think that I will live on so that his master plan will not come to light? Good-bye.

Chronic alcohol abuse

In Western countries, 33–70% of young suicides had abused alcohol or drugs (Shafii et al., 1985; Schuckit and Schuckit, 1989). Unlike in the West, chronic alcohol and drug abuse were not considered to be important factors found associated with suicides in Asian countries and with young Chinese suicides in Singapore. In fact, in Singapore (1969–76), there was no case of young suicide found associated with chronic alcohol abuse.

Alcoholism has never been a social or medical problem in the Chinese society (Shen et al., 1981; Lin, 1985; Kua et al., 1990). It has been said that the Chinese are highly sensitive to alcohol and have low tolerance due to genetic peculiarity (Lin, 1953). Chen et al.(1991) reported that the fast flushing response due to deficiency of ALDH-I activity may be the effective protective mechanism in Chinese against developing alcoholism.

The Chinese generally drink only with meals and on ceremonial occasions and the absence of popular drinking places in Chinese populated countries discourages the regular and excessive consumption of alcohol.

The Chinese reject alcohol-induced behaviour. In Hong Kong, Singer and Wong (1973) found that the Chinese alcoholics in Hong Kong showed certain differences from their Western counterparts. The Chinese were more introverted and neurotic and less aggressive in terms of violent tendencies or crimes of drunkenness.

It is possible that with time, as more adopt a Western lifestyle, there might be an increase in alcohol consumption of young Chinese leading to alcoholism. Concerns to this effect have been expressed in Hong Kong (Lee, 1980) and Taiwan (Hwu et al., 1995). However, community surveys carried out in Vancouver (Shen et al., 1981; Lin and Lin, 1982) and in mainland China (Shen, 1987) showed no noticeable increase in alcoholism among the Chinese.

Methods

In Singapore and Hong Kong, jumping from a high-rise is now the most important method of suicide adopted by the young Chinese. In Singapore, 75% of the young Chinese suicides jumped to their deaths from high-rise flats (table 5.5).

The most common methods of suicide adopted (for all age groups) in Taiwan are poisoning and hanging. Poisoning accounted for over 60% of all suicides in Taiwan. Suffocation by gases, cutting/slashing, jumping from high buildings and drowning are less common. Suicide by shooting or explosive is very rare in Taiwan (Chong and Cheng, 1995).

The Malays

The Malays originated from Southeast Asia. They migrated, in 2000 BC, to the coastal parts of Malaya and mixed with other races, the Chinese, Indians, Arabs and Siamese, to evolve into the modern Malays who now populate both Malaysia and Singapore (Hughes, 1965). In Singapore, about 14% of the population are Malays (1995). Almost all Malays are Muslim.

Little has been written on Malay suicide. However, Chen (1969), Chia (1978), Hassan (1983) and Kok and Aw (1992) in Singapore and Teoh (1974) in Malaysia have reported that among the three ethnic groups living in these countries, the Malays have the lowest suicide rate. The suicide rates in Muslim countries are also low ranging from 2 in Jordan (1975), 3 in Kuwait (1972), 5 in Egypt (1978), and 6 in Iran (1972) (Headley, 1983).

In the early days, the Malays in Singapore lived in atap houses in kampongs. Many of the Malays now live in subsidized high-rise flats in housing estates. In Singapore, unlike in Malaysia, the Malays do not have special consideration for places in the university, for jobs and for economic survival.

As the Singapore suicide statistics are reliable (Chia, 1978), these low Malay suicide rates are not an artifact. The strong condemnation of suicide by Islam must have a strong influence on the Malay suicide rates. However, it would be interesting to see how the Malays in Singapore cope with life stresses and with living in modern Singapore.

Religion and culture

Islam teaches its followers that life is the most valuable gift man possesses. Because it is a gift from God, it must not be taken away. To kill is bad but it is even worse to take one's own life. Life to the Muslim is a period of preparation for the hereafter. Life is a series of suffering. It is transient but the hereafter is permanent. Malays should not commit suicide under whatever circumstances. Also, those who commit suicide are a cause of shame to surviving relatives.

It is important to note that Islam's Shariah (law) 'covers not only public and private laws but also the ritual requirements which extends to cover all ethical and personal decisions and actions ...' (Taylor, 1975).

Thus, the daily life activities of the Malays are strongly influenced by their religion. Of significance to suicide are the laws on marriage, divorce and adultery; management of money; and on alcohol and gambling.

In the Malay society, the wife is subservient to her husband. Yet, it has been said that in almost every Malay household, a wife has at least as much authority as her husband and frequently more. Malay women would prefer to live on inadequate and infrequent meals rather than remain married to men who give them ample housekeeping money and who treat them well but whom they have grown to dislike strongly (Djamour, 1959). The Malay saying, 'What is the use of a full belly when the heart is sad' is pertinent.

Also, in the Malay society, there is a strong tradition to protect and support women and to behave kindly towards them. A woman can always depend on her own kin. The divorce rate among Malays is high. However, though divorce does mean serious hardship to the Malay women, they will adopt a confrontational attitude towards their husbands and in marital arguments they will seldom yield to threats (Djamour, 1959). With such an attitude and emotional support from her family and the society, a Malay woman faced with dispute or marital/family problems need not think of suicide as a solution.

Personal happiness is most important to the Malays. It permeates all fields of human behaviour. Their primary consideration in life is not so much the material advantage to be gained as serenity of mind. Immediate emotional security or contentment is more important than the prospect of practical advantage in the years ahead. Malays accept everything, whether good or bad, with unprotesting tolerance and resignation. Failure is accepted. The common Malay proverb, 'One's lot of a quart never becomes a gallon' beautifully describes this mentality. Malays are easy-going and tolerant (Mahatir, 1970). In Singapore, no Malay suicide was found preceded by job/financial problems or poor examination results.

In Singapore, compared with other ethnic groups, the Malay suicides were also found to be less frequently associated with physical illness. A Muslim prays five times a day and fasts for one month a year. Such practices would strengthen his self-discipline, tolerance for physical discomfort/pain and his faith.

Muslims consider alcoholic drinks unclean. Among the different ethnic groups in Singapore, the Malays have a larger proportion of young who abuse illegal drugs. However, there was only one case of young Malay male suicide who abused illegal drugs (marijuana) in Singapore (1969–76).

The Malays face the world with the help of their religion. Life is precious and must be lived to its natural end. No suffering is unbearable and no problems are insoluble, and suicide is never the answer. Also, to a Muslim, there is no escape from this world of suffering for the alternative is hell in the next world.

Death to all holds unknown fears. The Malay solves his problem by being resigned to his own death and seeks solace in prayers. He leaves himself completely at the mercy of his God. He and his close ones without much ado accept death when it comes. Malays do not commit suicide because of bereavement.

In conclusion,

1. The Malays are religious and Islam touches all aspects of their lives. Their needs are simple. Thus, life becomes less complicated and relatively free of personal conflict and burden.
2. The religious approach to life, though it dampens progress, competition and ambition, cuts out anguish, jealousy, envy and suffering. Pleasure, whether physical or mental, is considered as base. While alive, it is a duty to be of service to their fellow men.
3. The Malay customs consider women the weaker sex but have provided for them support when they are in trouble. Their training from young also makes it possible for them to accept divorce from their husbands without shame. Divorce rather than an unhappy marriage is the answer and is acceptable. There is, therefore, for them less necessity to maintain appearance for the benefit of their relatives or the public. This attitude towards marriage eliminates unnecessary misery and constraint.

   It might be said that among the three ethnic groups in Singapore, the Malays have more effective social support systems.
4. Finally, their religious practice of fasting every year for one month increases their tolerance for physical discomfort.

Why do young Malays commit suicide?

Malays in Singapore killed themselves when faced with love problems (19.5% of total suicides).

Love problems

A 17-year-old Malay male labourer. His father was a security guard. He jumped from a high-rise flat. He wrote:

Please dear, I hope you will not feel sad. Treat this matter calmly. I know that your family does not approve of our association because I am Muslim and you are Hindu. Please continue your studies at the university. Dear, please forget me as I wish to go far away from here. Good-bye.

Dear, I am doing this in order to make you happy and I do not wish to interfere in your studies. My life has become meaningless. This is why I wish to be away from you.

Mother, please forgive, forgive me all my sins. I am going far away from here because my life is always empty.

Malays also committed suicide because of severe mental illness – schizophrenia (36% of total suicides).

Trends

In a study of suicide in Singapore (1969–76), Chia (1978) found that there were altogether only 36 cases of Malay suicides (2% of total suicides in Singapore during this period). Twenty cases (56%) were below the age of 24, 11 cases were from the 25–44 age group (30%) and 5 cases were from the 45–59 age group (14%). There was no case above the age of 60. A study of Malay suicides in Singapore would therefore be mainly a study of suicides in the younger age groups.

Chart 5.3 traces the trend of Malay suicides in Singapore from 1959 to 1997. From the chart, it can be noted that the total suicide rates for Malays in Singapore are increasing. However, in the breakdown of Malay suicide rates by sex, it can be noted that the increase in rates are found more for Malay females than for males.

During this period, the male to female ratios of Malay suicides varied from 4.1:1 in 1959–63 to 0.7:1 in 1994–97.

The total suicide rates of the Malays in Singapore appear to be increasing. Will the total Malay suicide rates in Singapore continue to increase? This would depend on whether Islam and the various support systems in the Malay community could continue to protect the Malays in Singapore from the many rapid changes and stresses of modern city life. This deserves further research attention.

Chart 5.3: Trend of Malay suicide rates by sex in Singapore

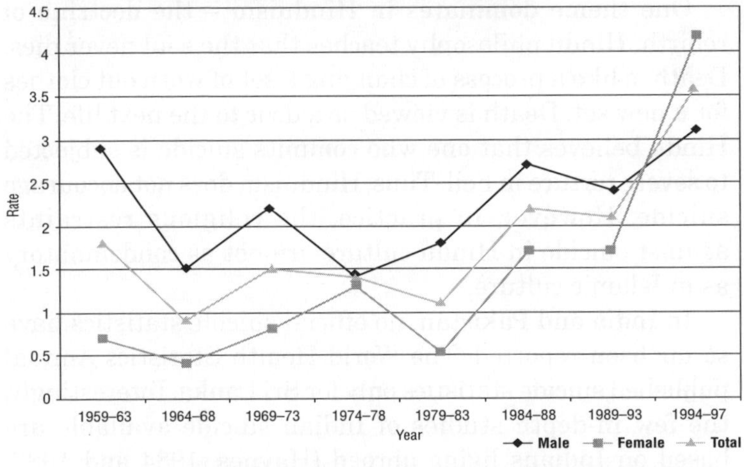

Source: 'Reports on Registration of Births and Deaths 1959–1997'. Registry of Births and Deaths. National Registration Department, Singapore.

The Indians

In India, in the early Vedic period (4000–2000 BC), the killing of self was permitted. In the later Upanishadic period (approximately 800 BC), however, the sacred writings strongly condemned suicide in the strongest terms:

> He who takes his (life) reaches after death the sunless region covered with darkness.

In Dharmasastras, suicides were permitted in some circumstances: suicide by an ascetic practicing self-starvation, suttee and mass suicide (women killing themselves to avoid humiliation and molestation by invading armies) (Bhatia et al., 1987).

One theme dominates in Hinduism – the doctrine of rebirth. Hindu philosophy teaches that the soul never dies. Death is like a process of changing a set of worn out clothes for a new set. Death is viewed as a door to the next life. The Hindu believes that one who commits suicide is subjected to severe torture in hell. Thus, Hinduism does not encourage suicide. However, in practice, the religious restraints against suicide in Hindu culture are not as condemnatory as in Islamic culture.

In India and Pakistan, no official suicide statistics have so far been reported. The World Health Statistics Annual published suicide statistics only for Sri Lanka. Interestingly, the few in-depth studies of Indian suicide available are based on Indians living abroad (Haynes, 1984 and 1987; Raleigh et al., 1990; Raleigh and Balarajan, 1992).

In Singapore, 6% of the population are Indians. The main practicing religion of the Indians in Singapore is Hinduism.

Patterns

In Singapore, compared to other ethnic groups, young Indians, especially young Indian females, had the highest suicide rates. In an age breakdown, the Indian female suicide rates peaked at the 10–24 and 65+ age groups but the Indian male suicide rates in Singapore peaked at the 25–44 and 65+ age groups (table 5.4).

Among the 10 to 24-year-olds, the Indian females in Singapore had a much higher suicide rate than the Indian males. For the 10–24 age group, the male to female ratio was 0.5:1 (reverse). Raleigh et al. (1990) also found that in England and Wales, Indian suicide rates were significantly higher among young females.

Table 5.4: Indian suicide rate by sex and age group in Singapore (1990)

Age group/Sex	Rate		'Male to female ratio'
	Male	Female	
10–24	12.5	26.5	0.5:1
25–44	30.5	26	1.2:1
45–64	10	–	–
65+	50	35.3	1.4:1

Rate: No of suicides per 100,000 population per annum

Why do young Indians in Singapore commit suicide?

Among the young Indians in Singapore, the females had much higher suicide rates than the males. Why?

In the Indian culture, females were from young brought up to be passive, docile and non-assertive. They are often downtrodden, devalued and considered burdensome (Hassan, 1983; Mehta, 1990). Sons, not daughters, are preferred in Indian society. Also, when provoked by the unreasonable expectations of their parents, their husbands or in-laws, the young Indian females are often not supported by their family or their society (Kakar, 1978).

Marriage must be arranged and approved by elders in the family, resulting in much stress and humiliation for the young Indian females who were rejected. Young Indian females, when cornered, would use suicide as an option to seek freedom from emotional pain and suffering.

Life for young Indian females can be difficult. The precipitants for young Indian females in Singapore were mainly family, marital and love problems (Chia, 1981).

Marital problems

A 24-year-old Indian housewife jumped from her high-rise flat after throwing three of her children down. In a letter tied to her wrist, she wrote:

I do not wish to live. No one is responsible for the death of my three children and myself. It is I who threw them down from above. I too jumped and committed suicide. No one should regret my action. I think that this is my lot and forget.

Love problems

An 18-year-old unemployed Indian female. Her parents objected to her boyfriend. She jumped from a high-rise flat. She wrote:

Dearest father and mother,

By now you will know everything. Mother you have brought me up showering me with much love and care. Thank you very much. I do not want to be a burden to you anymore.

Please do not blame my girlfriend for accompanying me to .... 's house. It was I who persuaded her to do so. No one is responsible for my death. I am sorry to disgrace our family. Do not worry about me. Bring up my younger sister in a proper manner. Sister, you must obey your parents.

Your loving daughter

For the young Indian male suicides, the precipitants were mainly love problems, job/financial problems, national service and problems with the law (Chia, 1981).

Love problems

1. A young male Indian. He hanged himself. He wrote:

To whom it may concern,

My death has nothing to do with anyone. I gave myself to someone without realizing that she does not even have the slightest interest in me. It is no use to live in this world without her. Please do not bother about my death and do not trouble anyone. No one cared for me when I was alive, they should be happy when I am dead.

2. A young Indian policeman. He shot himself. He wrote:

I love you very much and you love me very much too. I know. I have told you that I will only marry you or be a bachelor for the rest of my life. This is true. I prove to you what I have said. They think that my status is too low to marry you.

Young Indian males were romantic and steadfast in their love affairs. They would sometimes willingly prove their sincerity with their lives.

Suicide letters

In Singapore, higher percentages of young Indian than Chinese suicide letter-writers (table 5.2):

1. Expressed emotions – both negative (anger/hate) and positive (gratitude).
2. Left behind instructions to allay the anxiety and anguish of those left behind.
3. Bade farewell to loved ones and tried to exculpate others.

However, unlike the Chinese, the Indian young letter-writers did not say that they had not been filial or that they had to repay their parents for their upbringing. One young Indian wrote his last will.

Last will

A 24-year-old unemployed Indian male. He had financial problems. He wrote his last will before jumping from his high-rise flat:

I, ... IC No .... hereby authorize the following persons to my entitlement for my property and this is my last will.

My insurance life policy is be given to my beloved wife and son. But before she gets the money the proper authority will have to pay my debts to the following persons:

My father	$ 300
My mother-in-law	$ 500
My boss	$ 200
etc	$3075
Subtotal	**$4075**
My loan from insurance	$1000
Interest	$100
Total	**$5175**

The balance of my money is to be given to my wife. It is to be equally divided bewteen my wife and son. My son's money has to be put in a fixed deposit account at my wife's discretion. Regarding my furniture, my wife will have to say what she likes to do with them.

Yours sincerely, ...

Methods

Compared to other ethnic groups, a higher percentage of young Indians in Singapore hanged themselves (table 5.5). In India, different researchers come up with different findings with regards to frequency of different methods adopted. However, the common methods mentioned were poisoning (insecticides), hanging, burning oneself with kerosene, and jumping in front of an oncoming train (Rao, 1983).

Table 5.5: Method of suicide adopted by different ethnic groups in Singapore (1990)

	%		
Method/ethnic group	**Chinese**	**Malay**	**Indian**
jumping from high-rise flat	75	75	50
hanging	22.7	–	33.3
poisoning	2.3	10	16.7
others	–	15	–

6
Suicide Letters

In suicide, it is not possible to interview the subject personally. The stressful life events or situations leading up to the suicide can be documented retrospectively by interviewing the victim's relatives or by reviewing medical/ psychiatric records. But the actual emotional state and cognitive style of the suicide victim prior to the act can only be understood by analysing the contents of the suicide letter/s that he leaves behind.

There have been few attempts to analyse these writings, probably due to the practical difficulties involved in obtaining them. Some letters might have been written but destroyed by loved ones.

Also, not all suicide victims wrote letters. One must be literate before one can write letter/s. Those who were impulsive had no time to complete their letters. A few left behind letters because they were angry and wanted revenge. Thus, those suicides who left behind letter/s may not be typical of an average suicide (Heim and Lester, 1990).

In Singapore, there were previous studies done on suicide letters. Chia and Tsoi (1979) did a preliminary study on 266 suicide letters collected from the coroners' case-files. Hassan (1983) examined 26 suicide letters to study the cause of suicide in Singapore. In Sri Lanka, Dissanayake and Padmal De Silva (1983) reported that 18% of suicides left behind letters. Revenge, remorse and guilt were often expressed in their letters. The letter-writers asked for forgiveness. There was also a reference to a future that reflected the concept of rebirth found in Buddhism and Hinduism.

In Norway, Retterstol et al. (1985) reported that most of the suicide letters were friendly in nature and expressed gratitude to parents. Many of these letters also had a religious content and the victims expressed the hope that God would forgive them and that they would see their families again in heaven. All letters were short.

In contrast, the letters written by the young suicides in Singapore were not short. One letter contained 4595 words. A few of these letters were revenge letters, which were nasty. In Norway, Retterstol (1993) also reported that a motive of revenge often played a part. People took their lives 'over the head of their enemies' so that difficulties could be put in the path of the enemy later.

How many suicides left behind suicide letters?

In Singapore, 23% of young suicides left behind suicide letters, males more so than females. In the West, Capstick (1960), Poteet (1987), Thompson (1987) and Hoberman and Garfinkel (1989) reported that 15–24% of suicides left behind notes.

Thus, the percentage of young suicides who left behind suicide letter/s in Singapore is as high as those in the West. The percentage of letters written by young suicides may correspond with the literacy rate of the young in the country.

Do suicides who leave behind suicide letters differ from those who do not?

When the demographic variables of suicides in Singapore who had left behind suicide letters and those who had not were compared, it was found that significantly more of those who were young, single and who poisoned themselves left behind letters.

In the West, Heim and Lester (1990) found that those who left letters were more likely to be female, elderly, widowed and who used poison. However, Capstick (1960) found that those who left letters were younger. Tuckman et al. (1959) found that they differed only in the methods used to kill themselves.

Thus, different researchers from different countries come up with different findings.

Why did the young suicides in Singapore leave suicide letters?

In Singapore, young suicides wrote suicide letters:

1. To explain to their survivors why they had to kill themselves.

   As shown in table 6.1, 57% of young letter-writers gave reasons for the suicides. The reasons given were relationship problems (mainly love), job/financial problems, social problems and illness.

   About 17% of the letter-writers also stated that they had to kill themselves because their sufferings had become intolerable and would remain unabated (table 7.1). There was a sense of hopelessness. Life had become difficult and meaningless. About 17% of writers expressed a desire to leave this cruel world for a better next world.

   A small per cent felt the inevitability of death.

Death is inevitable

A 24-year-old Chinese male accountant. He took an overdose of barbiturate. He wrote:

The means of suicide – about 150 sodium amytal, 20 soneryl and beer. The only reason for my action is this –

Table 6.1: Content of suicide letters by age group (1969–76)

Content/Age group	No (% of total) suicide letters 10–24 (n=86)	25–85 (n=188)	
Reason for suicide	**49 (57%)**	**104 (55.5%)**	
relationship problems	28 (32.5%)	26 (14%)	x2 = 11.9, df 1, p<0.001
job/financial problems	15 (17.5%)	36 (19%)	
illness	12 (14%)	50 (26.5%)	
social problems	5 (6%)	19 (10%)	
Emotion	**49 (57%)**	**70 (37%)**	
gratitude	5 (6%)	22 (11.5%)	
anguish/despair/depression	32 (37%)	23 (12%)	x2 = 21.2, df 1, p<0.001
anger/hate	16 (18.5%)	16 (8.5%)	x2 = 5, df 1, p <0.05
revenge	4 (4.5%)	9 (5%)	
Instruction	**39 (45.5%)**	**98 (52%)**	
concern for others/allay	28 (33%)	69 (46.5%)	
corpse	15 (17.5%)	36 (19%)	
possessions	13 (15%)	31 (16.5%)	
last will	2 (2.5%)	7 (3.5%)	
Ask forgiveness	**28 (32.5%)**	**39 (20.5%)**	x2 = 3.85, df 1, p<0.05
Farewell	**28 (32.5%)**	**26 (14%)**	x2 =11.9, df 1, p<0.001
Exculpate	**7 (8%)**	**49 (26%)**	

DEATH IS INEVITABLE SOONER OR LATER. WHY NOT NOW?

I regret I did not go earlier. I am ashamed of my sinful thoughts, desires and ways and I ask you all and especially you the 'Creator of all' to forgive me. I thank my parents and the 'Great Creator' for this beautiful experience of life.

God Creator, forgive your child. Do not lose me. I love you.

Others said that they did not want to be a burden to their close ones or that they wanted to reunite with a loved one who had passed away.

Reunion suicide

A 17-year-old Chinese female domestic worker. She had lost her job. She became worried and depressed. She jumped from a high-rise flat. She wrote:

Grandma, I want to be with you.

(Attached to her suicide note was a photo of her grandmother who was deceased).

2. To express their deep (negative and positive) emotions.

   In Singapore, only 6% of the writers expressed gratitude, 30% expressed anguish/despair/depression, and 18% expressed anger/hate. Five per cent wrote 'revenge letters'.

Revenge

A 24-year-old male accountant. He took an overdose of barbiturate. He wrote:

You are the Macbeth and his wife of today. Why did you pick me as your victim? Or did you pick your victim at random and I happened to be the unlucky one? To let everyone know the exact story and how vicious and wicked you and your wife are, I will write my story .... What have I done to both of you? I gave you what you demanded. You swindled me. Your six months with me is like striking a lottery.

Yet you want to see me dead.

I never imagine a person can be so unprincipled, to the extent of telling lies to achieve their evil aims. I was too stupid to be so easily taken in by your lies and false pretense. Your name stinks. I die my dear .... not because of your threats. I die because of my anger at my own stupidity. It is also a good way to expose you otherwise there will be more victims like myself. I wanted to murder you and your wife and bring both of you with me. But that is too easy a way out for you. You will never live in peace anyway. My soul will haunt you forever wherever you go. You owe me a debt which I will collect from you when you come to join me.

In the United States, it was reported that 23% of young suicide victims left behind hostile suicide letters (Shaffer, 1974). The motive of revenge also played a part in suicide written by those in Norway (Retterstol, 1993).

3. To leave instructions for their survivors.

The writers (45%) still had concern for their close ones left behind. They tried to relieve them of anticipated grief or losses caused by their suicides. They wrote to say that they were happy to die as they would be going to a better place. They promised that they would bless, protect and repay their close ones from the place beyond.

Similarly in Western countries, Jan O'Donnel et al. (1993) reported that the letter-writers wanted their close ones to understand their actions and to forgive them. They tried to absolve others from any guilt they might feel and reduce the anguish of their next of kin.

Letter-writers also gave instructions on how to dispose of their possessions. Two wrote their last wills. Seventeen per cent of writers gave specific instructions with regard to disposal of their corpses and the types of funeral they should have. A few said that they wanted their bodies to be cremated and the ashes thrown into the sea. A few writers said: 'No postmortem please'.

4. To ask for forgiveness.

   Thirty three per cent of letter-writers (Chinese) asked forgiveness from their parents. They felt that they had not been filial and regretted that they were not able to repay their parents for their upbringing.

   Confucius's concept of filial piety (Rin, 1975) states: 'Serve one's parents when alive, bury them when dead and sacrifice to their spirits later.'

5. To bid their relatives a final farewell.

6. To exculpate others.

   In Singapore, suicide attempt is still a crime punishable by law. To exculpate their relatives from being accused of abetting the crime, letters were written to the authorities or police asking them not to further investigate the case and not to give their relatives further problems.

Exculpating others

One young Chinese suicide victim wrote:

I am ending my life on my own accord. My suicide has nothing to do with others. I, hereby, made this declaration so that the police can save much effort in their investigations. However, if the police have to find out the motives for my suicide, I will list them as follows: ....

Comparison of the contents of letters written by young and old suicide letter-writers in Singapore

From the tables 6.1 and 7.1, it can be noted that higher percentages of young than older suicide letter-writers:

1. Expressed their deep feelings of anguish/despair/depression and anger/hate.
2. Gave 'relationship problems' as a reason for their suicides.

3. Said that their 'present world' had become too intolerable and difficult and felt that the 'next world' would be better.
4. Blamed themselves and others.
5. At the time of death, were still deliberating.
6. Asked for forgiveness from their parents and bade them a final farewell.

In Singapore, about one quarter of the young suicides wrote suicide letters. The young letter-writers in their own words and style expressed their deep emotional feelings. They gave reasons for their suicides, which when compared to those found for the older letter-writers were not as devastating and often not multiple. Most importantly, they were at the time of death still reluctant to die as they were still deliberating.

Therefore, theoretically, it would be easier to prevent the young than the old from committing suicide. In prevention of young suicide, it is most important to delay them from harming themselves by supporting them emotionally during the crisis period. Alleviate their suffering. Help them to resolve some of their problems by correcting their negative way of thinking. With time, their crises will often resolve, and with therapy, their negative feelings will dissipate and their will to live will return.

Suicide letters offer a window into the thinking and feelings that encompass the suicide act. They are valuable and fascinating documents and furnish important data and understanding to the study of suicide (Shneidman, 1976).

7
The Suicide Process

A suicide is often preceded by a long period of development which often has its origins in childhood. In the early years of the individual, interaction takes place between child and parents and also other significant others. It is during these first few years of life that the most important foundation in a child's personality development is laid (Pfeffer, 1985).

If the individual encounters love, understanding and care, then he is more likely to feel confident and secure later in life. Such confidence will enable him to be more able to tackle effectively the many problems of life that he may encounter. However, if instead the individual faces rejection, coldness and indifference, it would be more difficult for him to develop a harmonious personality structure. If detrimental, lasting emotional instability may form in the individual predisposing him to stressful life situations that can trigger suicidal behaviour. Thus, in the suicidal process, the personality makeup of the individual is most important.

No parental love

I am very sorry I have to leave this world. I find living very miserable. No one really understands me. Not one of you in the family understands me. I am quiet all the time because I just cannot communicate with you. Whenever a conversation begins, it will but end up in quarrelling and shouting.

Honestly, I like to inform you that I have never received parental love which is necessary for me in life. I have no one to talk to except friends. I do have a few sincere and good friends.

Since young, Mother scolded me in front of my sister and caned me in front of my brothers. Mother further scolded and said it was my fault. Mother treated me badly. There was the time when I did not have any boyfriend. She insulted me with vulgar and obscene language. Those words remain in my heart until today. Father, you understand the situation but you are too afraid of mother.

Mother was fierce. She shouted, insulted and scolded me. I kept quiet. Why? Because of my timid nature and because of previous experiences. As a child I was always threatened and told to keep my mouth shut. A child is sensitive and her subsequent behaviour will be determined by the way she was brought up. I tried to forget but I was always unfairly accused. I can recall all my past silent sadness. Mum would like to deny the 'scar' that she had inflicted in me but God knows.

A home is a place filled with love, understanding, warmth, guidance and parental concern. Rejected and disliked, the child will automatically seek love from outside with blind eyes.

Mum and dad, I strongly agree that as a child I had given all of you a lot of problems. I beg your forgiveness. I have been bad in certain ways, as I am not perfect. But I wished that you had bothered to understand my character, background and sensitiveness. Always understand and make your children feel that they belong. I am talking through personal experience.

Anyway, parents, that's all I can say before I leave. Forgive me for my errors. Thank for bringing me into this world. That's the end of .... She has been the black sheep of the family.

Best wishes and success to all in my family.

Also, when an individual lacks effective cognitive and coping or problem solving skills, he is more likely to find himself placed in intolerable life situations from which he can see no way out. He then gets depressed. His vision becomes tunnelled. Minor problems and difficulties become major ones. He then loses hope and finds life meaningless. Suicide may be the solution (Pfeffer, 1989).

The suicidal individual frustrated with insoluble problems would get angry. His anger may be directed at self, at fate or at others. He would blame them for his misfortune (table 7.1 and figure 7.2).

Blame self

1. I have used up all my family's savings to save the company but it is for naught. Tragedy and financial disaster. I feel cheated by others because of my inability to interpret the English words in legal matters. I am stupid. I was made a scapegoat – spending my money for the benefit of some people. My family's assets were tragically squandered. Please seek redress.

2. While alive, I have nothing. I am willing to be a ghost. As I am a useless person, I would rather die.

Blame fate

1. Fate decides my failure. It cannot be helped if I am so destined. With better fate, I hope my children will do well in their studies so that they will in future be able to strive and secure good positions in society.

For years, I have been earning a living with my hands. Because of frequent illness I often sweat profusely. I feel weak and giddy when I do minor work. When the weather is bad, I get rheumatic pain which I find unbearable. Man has to die one day.

2. Papa this is the last time I shall address you. I am very upset. I am very sorry. Do pardon me for not being filial. I have one request. Please do not allow the reporters to publish this in the newspaper. Do not rebuke anyone. Life and death are fated. Good-bye.

Table 7.1: Contents of suicide letters by age group (1969–76)

Content/Age group	No (% of total) suicide letters 10–24 (n=86)	25+ (n=188)	
Reason for suicide	**49 (57%)**	**104 (55.5%)**	
difficult world	15 (17.5%)	15 (8%)	
suffering	14 (16.5%)	44 (23.5%)	
next world better	14 (16.5%)	27 (14.5%)	
no hope	10 (11.5%)	28 (15%)	
man is mortal	1 (1%)	8 (4.5%)	
burden	1 (1%)	5 (2.5%)	
reunion	1 (1%)	2 (1%)	
Deliberation	**11 (13%)**	**6 (3%)**	$x2 = 8.04$, df 1, $p<0.01$
Reluctant to die	**13 (15%)**	**18 (9.5%)**	
Decided to die	**33 (38%)**	**102 (54%)**	$x2 = 1.34$, df 1, ns
Determined to die	**2 (2.5%)**	**5 (2.5%)**	
Blame self	**20 (23.5%)**	**32 (17%)**	
Blame others	**18 (21%)**	**28 (15%)**	
Blame fate	**5 (6%)**	**12 (6.5%)**	

Figure 7.2: The Suicide Process

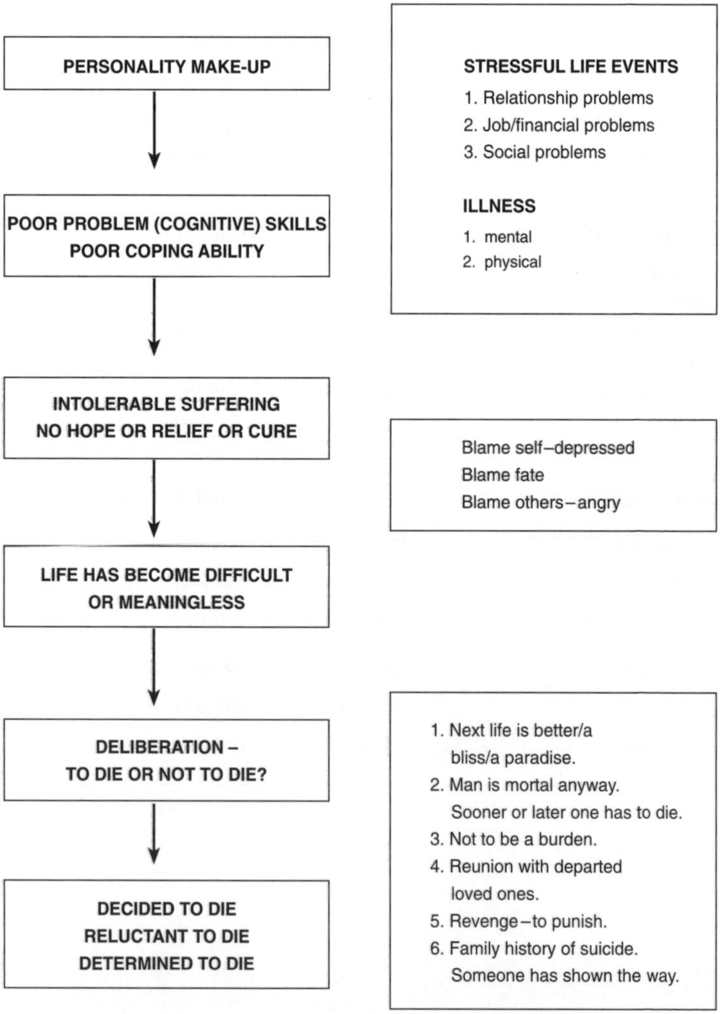

Many of the Chinese in Singapore still believe in reincarnation. According to this doctrine, an individual is subject to repeated cycles of birth and death before he achieves the ultimate salvation of nirvana. To the Chinese, if one has to suffer now it is probably because in the previous life one has done bad deeds. So it is one's fate that one must now suffer and one has to accept it.

Blame others

1. At work, I was scolded by my employers. They questioned me and scolded me nonstop. Now that I am dead they will be happy. I feel angry. Hypocrite! Pretend to be kind.

2. I hate this world. I have lost my husband and son. My husband did not understand me. My mother-in-law despises me. I am in great anguish. I want to die. When I die, I shall not think of them anymore.

Most suicidal acts of the young occur after some deliberation but a few may occur spontaneously and also a few may occur in a state of chaos or emotional confusion.

Emotional confusion

Finished. Everything is finished. Hopeless. Let me go. Why must my mind be filled with troubles? Do you know that if you have a troubled mind you should not be a policeman? Where to go? Do not want to go home. What have I done? Your belongings are mine. My belongings are mine. Why have we been acquainted with each other?

I have this 'agonizing enjoyment'. I like to be a sea gull. I do not know what is wrong with my mind. Without a love or a suitor. Nothing. Die. Someone is no good. Nothing can be done. Good-bye.

Thirty eight per cent of young suicide letter-writers stated in their letters that they had decided to kill themselves. However, even when they had decided, they would still at the same time be reluctant (Retterstol, 1993).

If someone in his family had committed suicide, the decision to proceed might be easier. However, if instead, they had to leave behind loved ones who needed looking after and if they felt they that they had been unjustly treated, then the decision to commit suicide would be even more reluctant and painful.

Reluctant to die

When you receive this letter I would probably have already left you. Please do not get sad about me nor too impulsive. Be calm. I will not put any blame on you even after I have left you. You have to understand my feelings. It is also difficult for me to take the full blame. I have suffered so much in my life and suddenly to meet one who could relieve my suffering. You just tell me how can I afford to let her go. How can I not love her deeply and with true passion?

I have no choice but to walk towards this path. Please do not keep this matter in your mind. You should forget me gradually and bravely. Never get sad about me.

Only 3% of letter-writers said that they were determined to die.

Determined to die

1. You will be shocked again when you received my letter. For the past 5 months, I have planned and this time I shall be 100% successful to fulfil my ambition. It is 100% foolproof. When you receive my letter, do not bother to ring me up for nobody will find me until such time.

2. I have taken poison. Please do not rescue me. If I do not succeed this time I will next jump from the highest building.

From the contents and cognitive style of the suicide letters, it is possible to hypothesize the mind-set of the young suicide victims. A better understanding of this mind-set can provide us with a foundation for devising effective cognitive strategy in the management of potential young suicide victims (Williams and Wells, 1989).

In cognitive therapy of young patient/client, the therapist must be aware of the patient/client's level of cognitive functioning, the specific cognition related to suicide, and how to alter this cognition (victim's negative cognition and cognitive rigidity). Of importance also are his negative feelings. Suicide may be construed as an end result of all these negative thinking and feelings, and the unavailability of sustaining support. Therefore, in therapy, one must correct the potential suicide victim's cognition, support him emotionally, and help him to adopt a positive outlook to life.

Are the suicides among the young an impulsive act?

In the West, it was reported that relatively few of the young suicides showed any evidence of preparation and planning for their suicides. They also showed fewer signs of having taken precautions against being discovered or to leave behind suicide letters. There was no evidence of a lengthy 'brooding' period before the suicides. All these suggested that the young suicides in Western countries were impulsive in nature (Hoberman and Garfinkel, 1989).

In Singapore, at a superficial glance, suicides of the young do appear to be impulsive in nature, especially when compared to those of the old. But, when these cases of young suicides were investigated in greater depth, it was often found that the stressful life events that they faced and their thought of suicide as a solution to them were not recent. In most cases, the final crisis appeared to be the final straw in a long history of personal unhappiness and grievances and behavioural problems.

8
Attempted Suicide

In studies of completed young suicide, a history of past attempts consistently stands out as an important risk factor. Shafii et al. (1985) believe that a past attempt is the single most important risk factor of suicide.

In Western countries, Shafii et al. (1985), Brent et al. (1988), Blumenthal and Kupfer (1988) and Farberow (1989) reported that 25–50% of young who completed suicide had made previous suicide attempts with the number of attempts and lethality of attempts positively correlating with ultimate suicide. In Singapore, Chia (1978) found that 15% of young suicides had past history of suicide attempt/s. In the case-notes of 25 young patients treated in a private psychiatric clinic who had committed suicide in Singapore, it was found that 8 (32%) of them had a history of suicide attempt/s.

In a follow-up study of 158 young suicide attempters treated in the same clinic in Singapore, it was found that 11 of them eventually committed suicide – 7% of total (5% for males and 8% for females). Follow-up studies of young attempters in Western countries reported that the rate of completed suicide was 9% for males and 4% for females (Kotila and Lonnquist, 1987).

Also, of 158 suicide attempters, the percentage of 'first-timers' who eventually committed suicide (7%) was higher than the percentage of repeaters (5%). However, in a 5-year follow-up study of adolescent attempters in Western countries, Kotila and Lonnquist (1987) found that the repeaters had a rate five times higher than that of the 'first-timers'.

Suicidal ideation or suicide attempt is a common psychiatric emergency encountered in clinical practices but is often unrecognized because the clinician who manages them is often inexperienced and has no skill in evaluating suicidal behaviour in the young. To be confident in conducting a meaningful interview with a suicidal young and finally to be able to effectively implement a strategy for intervention and follow-up, the clinician needs special education and training (Holinger et al, 1994).

In the West, Taylor and Stansfield (1984) revealed that 61% of their sample of suicide attempters did not comply with follow-up recommendations. They failed to keep their first appointment or dropped out of treatment after the initial assessment.

According to Trautman (1989), the reasons given were:

1. They felt that the attempt had served its purpose and the problems had been solved thus no further treatment was required.
2. They were afraid of being labelled as suffering from mental illness.
3. There was a desire of families to rationalize and deny serious problems and also there was a fear of disrupting an already tenuous family system.

9

Genetic Makeup and Contagion

Genetic makeup

In the West, family, twin and adoption studies have shown that there are genetic factors in suicide involving the transmission of mental illness (affective disorder and schizophrenia) (Roy, 1989). However, in adoption studies carried out in Denmark, Schlsinger et al. (1979) suggest that there might also be a genetic factor for suicide independent of or additive to, the genetic transmission of mental illness.

In Singapore (1969–76), there was an interesting case of family suicide suggesting that there might be more than one factor responsible for the suicides in this family.

Family suicide

In this family, there were three suicides including that of the deceased. There were also two others who had severe mental illness. Whether genetic factors for mental illness or for suicide played an important part in the suicides of several members in this family is worth debating.

The deceased was a 20-year-old Chinese female. The family stayed in a two-room HDB flat ,which they had rented for the past 6 years. Her father, 70, never supported the family financially. The mother, 39, suffered from diabetes but had to work as a washerwoman to support the family.

She had 7 siblings.

1. Brother – he had been admitted to Woodbridge hospital previously.
2. Brother – he had also been admitted to Woodbridge hospital. He committed suicide.
3. Brother.
4. Brother – he had an accident when young and had to undergoa brain operation. He committed suicide.
5. Brother.
6. Sister.
7. The deceased.
8. Sister – she had received psychiatric treatment from the outpatient clinic.

In spite of all the illnesses and suicides in the family, the family was happy. There were financial difficulties but they were not in debt.

The parents described the deceased as a very pleasant girl. She was quiet, homely, reserved and hardworking. In school, she completed her secondary four. At home, she did much of the housework. She worked for the army as a clerk-corporal for two years. Her officer-in-charge tried unsuccessfully to date her. As punishment he assigned her extra duties. She could not cope with the work and became upset. She was, however, prevented from resigning because of her three-year contract.

One week prior to the suicide, she became depressed. She could not sleep and lost interest in everything. She never mentioned suicide. She wrote a suicide note saying that all members of her family had treated her well. She wished to die because she was depressed and could not sleep.

In a follow-up study of young suicides who had received treatment in a private psychiatric clinic in Singapore, it was reported that 16% of them had a family history of mental illness and/or suicide compared with 7.1% of the control. In the Western countries, Shafii et al. (1985), Blumenthal and

Kupfer (1988) and Roy (1989) reported that 25–50% of young who killed themselves had a family history of mental illness and/or suicide.

Brown and Linnoila (1990) found diminished hydroxy-indole-acetic acid (5-HIAA) in the cerebrospinal fluid of individuals who were not depressed but who were impulsive or sociopathic. They postulated that it was possible that the genetic factor in suicide was 'the inability to control impulsive behaviour' and they believed that mental illness, and overwhelming stressful life events served but only as a potentiating mechanic which triggered this impulsive behaviour (suicide).

Asberg et al. (1986) and Pickar et al. (1986) also mentioned that CSF 5-HIAA might have the potential for predicting both completed suicides as well as attempted suicide inpatients after discharge from hospital.

Contagion

Shaffer and Gould (1987) believe that besides genetic inheritance, one has to consider the effect of imitation or contagion. Suicide may be imitated, especially in the young. Some believe that romanticized treatment of suicide could stimulate self-destruction. Goethe's novel *The Sorrows of Young Werther* was accused of initiating waves of suicides, which followed its publication. The death of Marilyn Monroe was followed by a wave of suicides among her fans (Motto, 1970). The young seemed to be more vulnerable and impressionable than adults in the face of mass media influences.

Fortunately, in Singapore, contagious suicide is uncommon (Chia, 1978). However, in Singapore, certain methods of suicide were found to be contagious within a certain period of time.

Contagion by method

1. A young couple jumped from a high-rise flat. The couple suicide was publicized dramatically in the local newspapers. Two weeks later, another couple jumped from another high-rise flat. The coroners' records showed that since then, there has not been a single case of couple suicide for the past two decades.

2. A young couple drowned themselves at Pierce Reservoir with their wrists tied together. Again, this couple suicide was publicized dramatically in the local newspapers. Two weeks later, another young couple drowned themselves in a similar way in the same reservoir.

3. A Chinese woman threw three of her children down from her high-rise flat before jumping herself. This was publicized dramatically in the local newspapers. About two weeks later, an Indian woman threw five of her children down from her high-rise flat before jumping herself. A newspaper cutting describing the suicide of the Chinese woman was found in the possession of the Indian woman.

During the early years, the local newspapers in Singapore would dramatize suicides. Fortunately, in recent years, they have stopped such presentations. It is hoped that this policy will be maintained.

In the West, detailed research has been conducted on two aspects of suicide contagion: fictionalized TV portrayals of suicide and newspaper reports of actual suicides. Studies of fictional portrayals of suicide on TV have found data both supporting (Gould and Shaffer, 1986; Phillips, 1982) and contradicting (Phillips and Paight, 1987; Berman, 1988) the hypothesis that such TV shows are related to an increase in suicide. Similarly, some researchers support a relationship between media news reports of actual suicide and an increase in suicide rates (Phillips and Carstensen, 1986) while other works do not support the hypothesis (Kessler et al., 1988).

The relationship between mass media accounts of suicide (both fictionalized and non-fictionalized) and shifts in young suicide rate is at present extremely scientifically controversial. Perhaps, the most we can say, given the current data, is that some evidence suggest that exposing the young population to suicide through the mass media may increase the risk of suicide for certain susceptible individuals (Centers of Disease Control, 1988a).

According to Wasserman (1984) prominent display of suicide in the mass media could lead to a predictable increase in suicidal deaths mainly of young people during the one to two weeks period following the display. The increase was most marked when there were repeated showings of the news. What is also important is the amount of publicity devoted to the suicide story (Phillips et al., 1989).

10

Infanticide-Suicide and Suicide Pacts

Infanticide-suicide and suicide pacts, though rare in Singapore, are given much publicity when they do occur.

Why do individuals commit homicide? At the present stage of research, it would be naïve to believe that we know the answer/s. Lester and Lester (1971) believe that individuals who have experienced physical punishment during childhood (external restraint) will more likely commit homicide while individuals who have experienced psychologically punishment (internal restraints) will more likely commit suicide. In some Asian countries, other factors such as robberies and gang fights play important roles in cases of homicide.

Some believe that suicide and homicide belong to two different groups of population with some degree of overlap.

However, we do know that cases of infanticide-suicide and suicide pacts in Singapore are mainly motivated by feelings of despair (depressive disorder) and cases of murder-suicide are more often motivated by feelings of anger and hostility.

Infanticide-suicide

A study of the coroners' case-files (1960–76) showed that during this period, there were only six cases of infanticide-suicide (0.2% of total suicides). All the murderers were female (mothers). The age of the murderers varied from 23 to 46-years-old and the victims' age varied from 1 to 9-years-old.

Prior to their deaths, the mothers were found to be depressed. They committed the acts because they were convinced that their situations were hopeless. They also believed that inevitable catastrophe would befall their dearest ones. To save their loved ones from all these future horrors, they killed them first and then, themselves.

Infanticide-suicide

A 23-year-old Chinese female. She was the mistress of an Indian man and had two baby girls, 1 and 2-years-old. Because of her relationship with this man, the rest of her family disowned her. The Indian man, however, refused to marry her. She wrote:

Love you very much. Die but my love for you will never die. You can never give me happiness. No use to try. Best of luck to you and your Arab lover. Forgive me for taking your children along. We are the unfortunate ones. I prefer to die with my children and forget everything.

In the United Kingdom, Marzuk et al. (1992a) reported that murder-suicide was common in England. Also, it was said that about 33% of murderers in England completed suicide. Compared to the non suicidal-murderers, the suicide murderers were more often female, older and had fewer criminal convictions. They were less likely to use brutal methods of suicide. Their victims were more often close relatives (children). A large number of the infanticide-suicides in the United Kingdom were also motivated by feelings of despair rather than feelings of anger. In the West, suicidal women with diagnosable depressive disorder were less likely to kill their husbands but sometimes killed their children before making an attempt on their own lives (West, 1966; Palmer and Humphrey, 1980).

In Japan, mother-child suicide known as 'oyako shinus' is a type of suicide peculiar to the Japanese and had an age-old origin. It was reported that the close bond between mother and child was the basis for this type of double suicide in Japan. The 'enmeshment of the mother with the child' and the mother's tendency to view the child as an extension of her own ego were the important psychopathology in such cases (Yoshimatsu, 1992).

Suicide pact

Lovers often wish to die together to satisfy the fantasy of a reunion in paradise (Rin, 1975). The suicide pacts of lovers are rare in Singapore. There were altogether only nine such cases from 1938–67 (1% of total suicides in Singapore). The suicide pacts of non-lovers are even rarer in Singapore.

In Japan, suicide pacts (shinju) are remarkably common (Iga and Tatai, 1975). Kato (1969) reported 3.6% of total suicides in Japan were double suicides (1948–60). In India, in the city of Bangalore, Sathyavathi (1976) reported that 25% of the total suicides in the city were suicide pacts (spouses, lovers, friends and sisters). The reasons for the suicides were financial, marriage and family problems. Methods adopted included poisoning, hanging and drowning.

In the United Kingdom and Western Europe, Rosen (1981) reported that about 1% of total suicides were suicide pacts.

11
Methods of Suicide

Methods of suicide would include the most common – poisoning, hanging and drowning – to the most exotic and complicated such as hara-kiri or seppuku (Seward, 1968).

In the early years in Singapore (1931), the common methods used were poisoning, hanging and drowning. Now, the common methods used are jumping from a high-rise, hanging and poisoning. Unlike in Western countries, poisoning in Singapore has become less common. Other rarer methods used in Singapore include piercing/cutting, shooting, burning oneself, running in front of an oncoming motor vehicle or train, and gassing.

Lester (1990) reported that the common methods used in the West included hanging, poisoning, shooting (firearms), drowning, jumping from a height, gassing and cutting (table 11.1). In Asian countries, poisoning (Dissanayake and Padmal De Silva, 1983; Chong et al., 1992; Choprapawon and Visalyaputra, 1992; Suk, 1992; Fan et al., 1992) followed by hanging were the most frequent methods used. However, in Japan, hanging was the most common method used (Yoshimatsu, 1992).

The types of poison used in Asian countries would depend on those which are easily available in the countries. Rat poison, insecticides and acetic acid were poisons used in some of the Asian countries.

Table 11.1: Methods of suicide adopted in 17 countries compared with those adopted in Singapore (1980)

Country/method	Rate							
	Poisoning	Gassing	Hanging	Drowning	Shooting	Cutting	Jumping (height)	Others
USA	1.3	1.1	1.6	0.2	6.8	0.2	0.4	0.2
Canada	2.6	1.5	3.1	0.8	4.7	0.2	0.6	0.5
Venezuela	0.9	–	2.2	–	1	0.2	0.4	0.1
Belgium	4.5	0.3	9	3.3	2.6	0.2	1.3	0.8
Denmark	9.9	3.9	9.6	2.8	2.5	0.5	1.3	1.2
England & Wales	3.2	0.9	2.1	0.7	0.4	0.2	0.4	0.7
France	2.4	0.4	7.3	2.2	4.2	0.1	1	1.8
Fed Rep. Germany	5.1	1.2	8.9	1.1	1.3	0.3	1.4	1.6
Italy	0.7	0.2	2.6	0.8	1	0.1	1.6	0.4
Netherlands	2.3	0.2	3.9	1.9	0.2	0.2	0.9	1.4
Norway	3	0.6	3.3	1.2	3.1	0.3	0.5	0.5
Scotland	3.6	1	2.3	1.3	0.5	0.2	0.7	0.4
Switzerland	3.6	2.3	6.8	2.6	5	0.5	2.5	2.1
New Zealand	1.7	2	2.6	0.9	2.1	0.3	0.9	0.3
Australia	2.8	1.6	1.5	0.4	3.5	0.2	0.4	0.6
Mean rate (Western countries)	**3.2 (2)**	**1.1 (6)**	**4.5 (1)**	**1.3 (4)**	**2.6 (3)**	**0.2 (7)**	**1 (5)**	**0.8**
Japan	1.1	2	9.4	1.3	0.1	0.4	1.2	2
Singapore	**0.7 (3)**	**–**	**2 (2)**	**0.1 (4)**	**–**	**–**	**5 (1)**	**0.4**

Source: Lester D. Changes in the methods used for suicide in 16 countries from 1960–1980.
(*) ranking
Rate: No of suicide 100,000 population per annum

In Japan, a famous Japanese writer killed himself with sleeping pills and popularized this method in that country. In his note he wrote:

> My first concern was not to die easily. Hanging satisfies this purpose, but imagining the ugliness of myself hanged dead. ... I decided to use sleeping pills.

It has been said that the Japanese are strongly sensitive to appearance after deaths. In Norway, drug is the poison most commonly used. (Retterstol, 1993).

In Japan, jumping from a high-rise became prominent in 1903 when a Japanese college student jumped from Kegon Fall, leaving behind a philosophical Chinese poem. His suicide was extolled as the first suicide for the purpose of merging oneself with nature. In the next eight years, there were about 200 completed and attempted suicides at the same place. Another Japanese college student in 1933 jumped into the Mihara-yama Volcano. Iga (1970) reported that 944 pupils imitated her by jumping to their deaths from the same place. In Japan, jumping from high places is a popular method for young females. Yoshimatsu (1992) reported that more than half of them preferred such a method.

In Singapore, Hong Kong (Lo, 1992) and Malaysia (Ong and Yeoh, 1992), jumping from high-rises accounted for 80%, 40% and 20% of suicides in the respective countries.

In general, young males tend to use more violent methods such as shooting and hanging than young females. More young females than young males poisoned themselves (Hawton, 1986). However, in Singapore, more young females (90%) than males (58%) jumped from high-rises.

History of the methods used in Singapore

Hanging

In 1931, the most popular method adopted in Singapore was hanging with a high rate of 11.5 per 100,000 population per annum. The rates by this method then gradually dropped to a low of 1.8 in 1981 (table 11.2).

Poisoning

Also, in 1931, poisoning was an important method used in Singapore with a rate of 8. In those early years (1937–41), the Chinese in Singapore poisoned themselves with caustic soda (sodium hydroxide), tuba roots and opium.

In Singapore, up to 1941, the use and sale of opium was controlled. It was a government monopoly. However, though the sale was controlled, it was available. In 1946, there was a proclamation prohibiting the sale and use of opium except for medical purposes. This drastic law on opium control immediately pushed many of the opium addicts to kill themselves with opium. But, subsequently, as opium became less available, the number of deaths by opium overdose dropped sharply.

When the 'Poison (sodium hydroxide) Rule 1958' was enacted, it became illegal to sell sodium hydroxide (caustic soda) unless the purchaser held a permit to purchase it. This led to a sudden drop of suicide by caustic soda.

In recent years, suicides in Singapore poisoned themselves mainly with insecticide, methyl salicylate acid and drugs prescribed by their own doctors. However, poisoning as a method dropped to a low rate of 0.8 in 1991.

In Norway, of the total cases of poisoning, 94% were due to drugs. Antidepressants were the leading drugs used for committing suicide. Of the antidepressants used, amitriptyline topped the list followed by doxepin, imipramine and triimipramine (Retterstol, 1993).

Drowning

Singapore is a small island and there is easy access to the sea, reservoirs, or canals. A few suicides in Singapore submerged themselves in bathtubs filled with water. However, drowning/submerging is now no longer a popular method in Singapore. The rate by this method was a low of 0.1 in 1991.

Jumping from a high-rise

Compared to other countries, jumping from a high-rise as a method now ranks the highest in Singapore (table 11.1).

In the early years, there were few high-rise buildings in Singapore. Some of them included the Cathay building, Pickering HDB flat and Selegie HDB flat. During that time, people jumped from these buildings and the newspapers highlighted their suicides dramatically and repetitively. These locations and the method subsequently began to acquire an attraction and significance for potential suicide victims.

Similarly, in San Francisco, people travel to the Golden Gate Bridge to jump, illustrating the powerful significance that the bridge holds for them. Knowledge that it can be an effective or painless method may overwhelm the potential suicide's ambivalence about killing himself (Calvin, 1985).

In 1931, the suicide rate of jumping from a height in Singapore was only 0.2. This rate has since gone up to a high of 6.7 in 1991.

During the Japanese occupation, the building of new houses and the maintenance of old ones stopped almost entirely. In those days, the types of houses commonly found

Table 11.2: Trend of suicide rates by method adopted in Singapore

Year/method	Rate				
	Jumping (high-rise flat)	Hanging	Poisoning	Drowning	Others
1931	0.2	11.5	7.5	1.5	1.5
1941	0.5	5.5	5.5	0.9	0.9
1951	0.1	3	3.5	0.5	1.5
1961	0.9	4.5	1	1	0.8
1971	5	3.5	1.5	0.5	0.5
1981	5	2	0.7	0.1	0.4
1991	6.5	3	0.8	0.1	0.8

Source: 'Reports on Registration of Births and Deaths (and Marriages), 1931–91'.
Registry of Births and Deaths and (Marriages). National Registration Department, Singapore.
Rate: No of suicides per 100,000 population per annum.

on the island were bungalows, terrace houses, shophouses and atap roofed houses.

After independence in 1959, the Singapore government began to aggressively resettle squatters, demolish old buildings in the slums and build subsidized pubic housing. By 1978, 295,000 units had been constructed by the HDB (Housing and Development Board). Virtually all of the units constructed by the HDB have been flats, many in blocks of 25 storeys or more. About 85% of the population in Singapore now reside in such units. Now, about 70% of suicides in Singapore are by jumping from high-rises.

Stabbing/slashing, burning oneself, shooting, and gassing

Stabbing one's abdomen or slashing one's neck with a sharp knife was once a popular method adopted by the Chinese in Singapore. Burning oneself by kerosene was at the height of its popularity in 1969–70. During that period, much newspaper publicity was given to the self-immolation of South Vietnamese Buddhist Priests.

Suicide by shooting was only adopted by the police, armed forces personnel and criminals in Singapore. Only expatriate Caucasian women in Singapore committed suicide by gassing.

Methods used by the young in Singapore

The most common methods of deaths amongst the young suicides in Singapore are jumping from a high-rise and hanging. Fewer of the young suicides are by poisoning or drowning themselves (table 11.3). In Hong Kong (1989), 63% of young males and 100% of young females (10–19 age group) jumped to their death from high-rises (Shek, 1993).

Table 11.3: Trend of methods adopted by the young in Singapore (1969–76 & 1990)

	No (%)	
Method/Year	**1969–76***	**1990**
jumping from high-rise flats	74 (54%)	39 (69.5%)
hanging	11 (8%)	13 (23%)
poisoning	40 (29.5%)	1 (2%)
drowning	5 (3.5%)	–
others	7 (5%)	2 (3.5%)
multiple	–	1 (2%)
Total	137 (100%)	56 (100%)

* Source: Chia BH. *Suicide in Singapore*, MD thesis, Singapore, University of Singapore, 1976.

As the young in Singapore have little knowledge and access to lethal poison, to kill oneself by poisoning can be a slow and unpleasant process.

Suicide letter written of a young female who drank poison

Now, minutes have passed after I drank the poison. Why is there no unusual sign? I am very frightened. I want to die. I will have to succeed in my suicide attempt; otherwise I will have to jump down from the flat.

What I am afraid of is that the poison I have drunk will not kill me. Then, it will be miserable. Maybe, it has taken effect. Don't save me. My throat has already .... It is unbearable.

It is indeed frightening. Half an hour has passed and why has nothing happened to me, other than just feeling uncomfortable? Good heavens, let me die this afternoon to end this miserable life. I am determined to die. Maybe there is a slight effect now. I don't beg for any other thing but only for the success in this suicide attempt. What is detestable is that maybe the poison is mild and so it has very little effect.

Now it is 3.55 pm. I am still all right. There is little effect. Maybe I have drunk too little and so have to drink up what is left behind. However, I am a bit frightened. What can I do? If I don't die, it will be more terrible. I have to drink up what is left.

Alas! Good heavens! Now it is 4.20 pm. I don't feel much pain and then it is only a little bit of unusual feeling. It may be that I am frightened. If I don't die this time, then I pledge that I will by all means end this miserable life. It is now 4.30 pm. I have to succeed in this suicide attempt. No one should save me. Good heavens!

Now it is 4.40 pm. Only one hour and forty minutes after I have drunk the poison. Now I am only slightly frightened. The poison takes some effect psychologically. Perhaps I will die soon.

It is almost 5 pm and I am still alive but I am shivering. As I have lost hope in everything, I am going to die. Now it is 5.25 pm and I am still living in this world. I am now in a cold and gloomy world. I am not afraid of anything and only want to die. Only death will free me from all misfortune. Please let me die soon. I believe that it is the effect of the poison, otherwise why is there noise running through my body? I do not care for anything. I want to die. I want to die.

*Her body was found at 7.30 pm by her family.

In the United States (1990), Holinger et al. (1994) reported that 67% of the young suicides used firearms, 18.5% hanged themselves, 5.5% gassed themselves, 5% used drugs, 0.5% used poisons and 3.5% used other means.

The frequency of methods used by the young, like adults, varied greatly from country to country.

Jumping from high-rise flats in Singapore is common because:

1. Available/cheap method

As 85% of the population now reside in high-rise flats, jumping from a high-rise flat as a method is easily available. However, if availability is the only criterion, many would have stabbed, hanged, poisoned or drowned themselves.

In homes, knives are freely used and easily available if one wishes to use this method for suicide. Poisons commonly used for suicide in Singapore are freely sold in the open market. One can easily drown oneself in the sea around the island, in inland reservoirs and canals or in a bathtub. To hang, one only needs a rope and a quiet spot.

Thus, some methods, though easily available, are not used because deaths from such methods can be painful, slow and unattractive to the victims.

2. Fashion/preference

This is also important. A person contemplating suicide may be inclined to imitate the methods used by others. A method can be learned.

3. Knowledge and familiarity

Knowledge and familiarity with a method may influence the decision.

4. Lethal method

Jumping from a high-rise flat is a lethal method.

One method may be acceptable while another may not be. A lot would depend not on only one but multiple factors.

12
Bereavement

In the East, to date no study on bereavement from young suicide has been available. Chia (1978) in his psychological postmortem study of young suicides in Singapore interviewed 41 parents of young suicides 3 to 6 months after their suicides.

Seventeen percent of parents when interviewed were still 'shocked' and 'confused' 3 to 6 months after the suicides of their young (table 12.1). Seventy eight per cent felt very depressed because of the loss, 15% felt shameful, and 5% felt guilty. Seventeen per cent of the parents blamed others and 5% felt that neighbours were still gossiping about them. Interestingly, no surviving parents of the young suicides blamed the deceased.

Also, in the West, it is only in recent years that we see an interest in this area of study emerging (Holinger et al., 1994). Of great interest is whether the bereavement by parents from suicides of their young is different from that from a natural death or an accident. Cantor (1975) has suggested that the grieving process of parents following young suicide is qualitatively different from that of a natural death.

Clinical experience indicates that parents of young suicides would have great difficulty with guilt, shame and stigmatization, depression, somatization and other psychological traumas. Parents also more frequently reported a sense of failure in their parenting role. They

Table 12.1: Reactions of parents to young suicides (1974)

Reaction	No (%) Parent (n=41)
shock	7(17%)
why suicide?	5 (12%)
sadness	32 (78%)
shame	6 (1.5%)
guilt	3 (7%)
blamed others	7 (1.7%)
blamed deceased	–
indifferent	1 (2%)
felt evil spirits drove victim to suicide	2 (5%)
felt neighbours were gossiping	2 (5%)
refused to be interviewed	1 (2%)

Source: BH Chia. *Suicide in Singapore.* MD thesis, University of Singapore 1978.

might assume a degree of responsibility for the death that might be unrealistically self-punitive. All these make the effect of the unanticipated and unwelcome death very stressful indeed. It has been said that the relatives of suicides had their lives changed unalterably and against their wills (Holinger et. al, 1994).

The factors found specific to young suicidal death are:

1. The sudden, unnatural and unexpected loss.
2. The fact that the death is often violent.
3. The trauma associated with the discovery of an unsightly corpse.
4. The fact that the death is often preceded by disharmony within the family (family pathology).

Family members may blame one another, looking for a scapegoat. Also, police presence is prominent. To rule out homicide, the police investigating the case may take a more antagonistic position with the surviving family members. Newspaper reporters may ask insensitive and often accusatory questions. Few relatives will rush out to help. Under these circumstances, the grieving process of a suicidal death may be incomplete or unusual and social support may be found wanting (Dunne, 1992).

In the treatment of young suicides' parents, successful crisis resolution depends on early and effective crisis intervention. This is not the time to wait for parents to ask for help. In therapy, the therapist should focus on the immediate problem of dealing with the loss. The parents may need a variety of emotional support through the crisis following the young's suicide.

The possibility of depressive disorder and even suicide in surviving family members must be borne in mind. The short-term use of anxiolytics is helpful. It may take a lifetime for parents to get over the suicide.

13
Assessment

Suicide occurs infrequently in the young in Singapore and in all other countries. It is a complex psychosocial, cultural and medical problem. The causes are multiple and they interact. Also, there is no specific or unique feature found in a person who commits suicide. Assessment of suicide risk in the young is, therefore, never an easy task.

To be competent in the assessment, the assessor has to understand young suicide and the culture where it occurs. He also has to be skilful in interview techniques, tactful, sensitive and caring. The potential suicidal patient/client can be distressed, mentally abnormal, manipulative, uncooperative and demanding, making the task even more difficult. Thus, assessment of the danger of suicide in a young individual is one of the most difficult tasks in medicine and psychiatry. No one can be skilled enough in this assessment. However, it is possible to make oneself more skilled through experience and knowledge.

Suicide is a major legal problem for psychiatrists and mental health workers. In the United States, suicide is the number one legal claim against mental health professionals (Gutheil, 1992). In the United Kingdom, statistically, psychiatrists are a relatively 'low risk' specialty but no less than 50% of all claims/complaints made by patients against psychiatrists were related to suicide or attempted suicide (Brahams, 1991).

Risk factors

In Singapore, the risk factors are:

Demographic factor

1. The suicide rates of the different ethnic groups in Singapore are markedly different. Among the different ethnic groups in Singapore, young Indians had the highest suicide rate, the young Chinese had an average suicide rate, and the young Malays had the lowest suicide rate (Chia, 1978 and 1981).
2. In Singapore, young married females had higher suicide rates than young single females. Marriage did not seem to protect these young females from committing suicide. However, in Singapore, young single males had higher suicide rates than young married males.
3. The suicide rates for the unemployed young in Singapore were high for both sexes.
4. In Singapore, the main precipitants for young suicides were relationship problems, job/financial problems, and social problems. Compared to males, higher percentages of female suicides were precipitated by relationship problems.

   The types of relationship problems which precipitated the young suicides in Singapore included dispute/being reprimanded, love/marital/family problems, and bereavement. The types of social problems included job/financial problems for both sexes, national service for males, and poor examination results for females.
5. Young with a family history of mental illness and/or suicidal behaviour.
6. Young with knowledge and easy access to lethal methods of suicide.

Clinical factor

1. Personality disorder

Chia (1978) reported that the parents and relatives of the young female suicides frequently described them as being 'sensitive, stubborn and impulsive'. They were prone to mood swings, had a low sense of responsibility and commitment, and had low tolerance for suffering and hardship. A few of the parents of young male suicides described them as being antisocial.

Dissanayake and Padmal De Silva (1983) in Sri Lanka reported that their young suicides were described by their relatives as being 'stubborn and hot-tempered'. One was a lawbreaker.

2. Mental illness

In Singapore, about 23% of young suicides were associated with mental illness (more male and female). In the diagnostic breakdown, about 18% of the young suicides were associated with schizophrenia but only about 2% with depressive disorder. I believe that affective disorder was under-diagnosed among the young suicides in Singapore.

Comparing the demographic and clinical data of 'living and suicide young schizophrenics', significantly more of the 'suicide schizophrenics' were found with the following variables: being unemployed, being separated/married, presence of recent stressful life events, being depressed, past history of suicidal attempt/s, and having illness with recurrent relapses.

The other diagnostic categories of importance were paranoid and panic disorder. Only 1 case (0.7%) of young suicide in Singapore was associated with chronic drug abuse. No case of young suicide in Singapore was associated with chronic alcohol abuse.

3. Physical illness

In Singapore, only 7% of the total young suicides were diagnosed as suffering from physical illness (1969–76) (Chia, 1978).

4. Past history of suicide attempt/s

In Singapore, 15% of the total young suicides had a past history of suicide attempt/s. When the suicide attempters treated in a private psychiatric clinic were followed up (20 years), it was found that 7% eventually committed suicide.

Biological markers

The biological markers found associated with suicide were:

1. Variables associated with 5-HIAA

5-HIAA, a serotonin metabolite, was found to be low in the cerebrospinal fluid of patients suffering from depressive disorder. Asberg et al. (1986) found that those depressed patients with low 5-HIAA had an increased incidence of suicide attempts, were more determined in their attempts with preference for active or violent methods, and were more likely to die from suicide than those with a higher cerebrospinal fluid 5-HIAA.

2. Variables associated with release of cortisol

Bunney and Fawcett (1965) reported that patients who committed serious attempts or who committed suicide had an unusually high excretion of cortisol metabolites prior to the event. Carrol et al. (1982) and Banki et al. (1984) reported that a positive dexamethasone suppression test (DST) was related positively to suicide.

Linkowski et al. (1983) reported a very low response of thyroid-stimulating hormone (TSH) after the effect of thyrotrophin-releasing hormone (TRH) to be predictive of suicide.

3. EEG (Electroencephalography)

Strue (1986) reported that suicide attempts were positively associated with paroxysmal EEG dysrhythmia.

The results obtained from researches on 'suicide and biochemistry' and 'suicide and EEG', for the time being, have little or no practical application. However, it has been predicted that in the future they will represent a valuable supplement in the assessment of suicide risk.

Suicide prediction scales

The suicide scales frequently used are:

1. Beck's suicide intention scale (Beck et al., 1974)

Of the scales available, 'Beck's suicide intention scale' is the most useful. It is easy to administer and can be incorporated conveniently into one's clinical interview. High scale scores correlate with high suicide intent. Taken in isolation 'intention scale' would be of limited value but in combination with clinical findings, it can be useful.

2. Hopelessness scale (Beck et al., 1979)

About 12% of young suicide letter-writers in Singapore said that they committed suicide because they felt that their situations were hopeless. A measure of 'hopelessness' would be a good predictor of risk of eventual suicide.

Beck and his colleagues found a person's subjective expectations about the future (in this case hopelessness) were highly correlated with the seriousness of his suicidal intention. Beck et al. (1975) suggested that suicidal intent might be modified if the patient was systematically helped to revise his view.

3. Prediction scale

Pallis et al. (1982 and 1984) have developed a scale to predict successful suicide in people who had attempted suicide. The scale correctly classified 60% of suicide cases but mis-classified 26% of suicide attempters. Therefore, using this scale as a method of detecting suicide has practical limitations as the number of suicide attempters who would not eventually commit suicide is quite large and would overwhelm one.

Prediction of young suicide is difficult because:

1. Suicide is an uncommon phenomenon.
2. The suicide population is not homogenous.
3. The causes of suicide are multiple and they interact.
4. There is no specific/unique feature found in a person who commits suicide.
5. It is also difficult to predict what stressful life events or change of events a suicidal individual will face in future that might alter his suicide risk status.

Screening protocol

Although a great deal of effort has been expended in trying to devise a reliable and valid screening instrument, there is as yet no generally accepted instrument in widespread use. Yufit (1989) has described the difficulties of developing such protocol and made a plea for a major collaborative effort in the endeavour to develop a suicide-screening checklist.

At the present, there are no psychological tests which can predict with any degree of accuracy whether a person will commit suicide. Ultimately, it is the person giving treatment who must assess this on the basis of a comprehensive understanding of his patient, knowledge of the suicide patterns in the community, and the risk factors involved.

Assessment

In the assessment of suicide risk, one has to be comprehensive. Demographic and clinical information must be elicited. Such information of importance may vary from country to country and from culture to culture.

Also, of great importance is the interview technique. The interviewer has to be respected, knowledgeable, experienced, understanding, warm, tactful and patient. He should not be forceful in the examination but should try and achieve empathy, create understanding, warmth and affection and, if possible, develop a positive transfer relationship.

Above all, the interviewer must be prepared to hear suicidal thoughts and feelings and not be frightened by the expression of such wishes. Some interviewers may have anxiety about posing questions about suicide ideas and feelings because they are inexperienced and are not confident about what to do if a candidate should announce an intention to commit suicide. They do not want to hear about suicidal symptoms or work with candidates with suicidal ideas for fear that they may have to bear legal responsibility. Interviewers who are unprepared to hear or are frightened by these ideas and feelings cannot assess the degree of suicidal risk posed.

One has to ask direct or indirect questions on suicidality. However, one should obviously not rush blindly into the problem as one of the first things to be assessed. It is necessary first to get to know the patient and gain an insight into his life. Then gradually find out about previous attempt if any and about suicide ideas.

Studies done in Western countries among university students have shown that suicide ideas are prevalent even among the young. In a study to assess suicide idea and behaviour in a population of 1678 undergraduate students in Australia by the use of modified suicide ideation scale (SIS) and questionnaire, Schwetzer et al. (1995) found that 62% of the students showed some suicide ideas and 6.6% reported one or more suicidal attempts. Also, in the United States, Rudd (1989) and Dixon et al. (1992) reported that the prevalence of suicide idea among university students is high with estimates varying from 32% to 74%.

I have devised a 'suicide risk assessment protocol'. The main aim of this protocol is to make sure that the clinicians acquire all the relevant data pertaining to suicide risk for the cases that they manage. When used, it may also guide and prompt the clinicians, who may be inexperienced in this subject, to make judgment on the degree of suicide risk in the cases they manage.

In practice, most clinicians do not rely on epidemiological data in assessing suicidal risk nor do they use predictive scale. They instead use clinical criteria in assessing suicidal risk. As the current state of suicide prediction for an individual instance is still unreliable, and the consequence from errors in assessment can be fatal, a deviation from the normal practice may be required.

Also in assessment, many clinicians will either underestimate or overestimate the seriousness of the suicide ideas or behaviour. From knowledge and experience come humility and a better understanding of the difficulties one faces in this task.

After the assessment, the clinicians must document their findings. Gutheil (1984) said that documentation is the 'make or break' issue in liability case. However, more importantly, it is the nature and quality of documents that would finally influence the outcome of the liability case. Sloppiness and negligence in documentation are particularly damaging.

At the end of the day, the clinician has to give his final verdict of 'no risk, mild risk, moderate risk or high risk'.

Warning signs of pending young suicide

1. Young with certain personality makeup: asocial, stubborn, hot-tempered and impulsive (female) and young who are antisocial (male).
2. Young who are often angry and unhappy. They may have crying spells, poor appetite, loss of interest in daily activities, persistent insomnia, retardation/agitation, feelings of tiredness though having rested, poor concentration/ memory.
3. Young with feelings of helplessness and hopelessness. Life to them has become difficult and meaningless.
4. Young with difficulty in coping with life situations – school, national service (for boys), job, love and family problems.
5. Poor communication between the young and parents, other family members, and teachers, leading to isolation.
6. A family history of suicide and/or mental illness, or recent losses in life situations.
7. Young with abnormal signs and behaviour – laughing or talking to self, abnormal suspicions, threatening and/or aggressive behaviour (schizophrenia). They are often 'frightened'.
8. Young who abuse alcohol or illegal drugs.
9. Young who voice suicidal ideas, threaten suicide or attempt suicide.

10. The behaviour of young suggests to the parents that he is biding them a last 'farewell' (giving away precious possessions/contacting and wishing friends and relatives good-bye). Young write suicide letter/s.

Suicide Risk Assessment Protocol

Name:	Sex: m / f	Marital status: s / m / sep / div
Residence:	Age:	Occupation: ....
	Race:	Religion: ....
HDB flat: Yes / No	Place of birth:	Where assessed: ....
Residence:		Date: ....

Suicide idea or plan Yes / No

Presence of stressful life event 1. Days 2. Weeks 3. Months Type 1. Relationship problems: .... 2. Job/financial problems: .... 3. Social problems:	Previous suicide attempt Yes / No If Yes Use scale 1. Beck's suicide intention scale Score .... 2. Beck's hopelessness scale Score .... Availability of method Yes / No

Family history of mental illness
Yes / No

Family history of suicidal behaviour
Yes / No

Present of significant other
Yes / No

Support from family member
Yes / No

History of

1. Personality disorder

....

2. Alcohol/illegal drug abuse

....

3. Physical illness
   type of illness

....

Illness causing much suffering
Yes / No

Illness incurable
Yes / No

Current psychiatric diagnosis

....

Seen doctor/mental health professional in last month
Yes / No

Specify

....

Hospital admission

....

Response to treatment given
Good / Poor

Relapse
Yes / No

Overall Assessment Of Current Suicide Risk

1. None
2. Minimal
3. Moderate
4. High

14
Prevention

Research

In suicide prevention, it is important to study not only what causes suicide but also what prohibits suicide. The recognized factors which deter a potential victim from killing himself are religion, the fear of death, and having a meaningful or happy life. If one is committed to the world one lives in, one will be reluctant to leave it.

In Singapore, according to a survey done, about 73% of the Chinese followed the Chinese religions and 10% were Christians. Almost all the Malays were Muslims. Among the Indians, 71% were Hindu and 17% were Muslims. For many, religion supplies answers and explains the happenings and meaning of life (Nikkyo, 1975 and 1982). Man in this world often faces happenings over which he has no control. He feels helplessness. Religion may give a meaning to life and may bring peace of mind to one so troubled. It has been said that religion 'is ... born of the need to make tolerable the helplessness of man'.

Among the various religious groups in Singapore, Tamney (1969) and Wee (1976) reported that Muslims and Christians are more religious than the adherents of other religions. In Singapore, of the three ethnic groups, the Malays are found to be the least prone to suicide. For Malays, it is the genuine and conscientious daily practice of religion and remembrance of its various beliefs that probably give a Malay individual an extra dimension in the form of greater resilience and strength to withstand the vicissitudes of life and suffering. The Koran includes regulations governing marriage, divorce, food and many other aspects of daily life. Mohammed also prohibits gambling and alcohol. Also, the Koran forbids one to take one's life in the strongest terms. Religion plays a big part in suicide prevention for the Malays in Singapore.

To the Christians, life belongs to a supernatural power and death from suicide may lead to suffering, making suicide repulsive. The sixth commandment in the Bible states that 'Thou shalt not kill' which can be interpreted to mean that Christians should not take lives, be it their own or others'.

In the early years, the Christian's attitude towards suicide was very harsh. Suicide was regarded as committing a sin of the first magnitude. In the Middle Ages, the prevailing attitude towards suicide in European countries was condemning. Suicide was then an act condemned by the church. The three penalties imposed on those who committed suicide were confiscation of property, degradation of the corpse and refusal of burial in consecrated ground. However, in time, the right to die was placed in the hands of the individual. John Donne, a poet and the Dean of St. Paul's wrote 'Biathanatos', the first defense of suicide in English. Donne demonstrated that suicide is not incompatible with the law of God, reason and nature (Rosen, 1975).

In Thailand, the suicide rates are low. The dominant religion in Thailand is Buddhism. To every Thai Buddhist in Thailand, religion is important and relevant (Bussaratid and Ruangtradool, 1983). However, in Sri Lanka, also a Buddhist country, the suicide rates are high (Dissanayake and Padmal De Silva, 1983).

The other social factor that may need to be researched on in suicide prevention is the effect of the hasty implementation of radical and unpopular national policies on the population such as in China during the Cultural Revolution. Headley (1983) reported that suicide rates for certain groups of the population during this period in China increased dramatically.

National policies introduced by a government should be implemented humanely, carefully and gradually so as to inflict minimum suffering and hardship on the individuals in the population. There must be sufficient time to allow the individuals in the population to adapt to the change/s to be implemented so that tragic consequences would not be the result. Also, national policy if implemented with good intention but without an in-depth understanding of the country's population and economic statistics and culture could lead to disastrous consequences as in Sri Lanka.

In Sri Lanka in the early years, the traditional centre of learning in the village was the Buddhist temple, where the vernacular was taught and Buddhist ethics were explained. Under the British administration (1815–1948) it was reported that the stability of the old system was shaken to its foundations. Free and compulsory education was introduced in 1947 and mass education was introduced in schools controlled by the government or by Christian missionaries.

A new caste, the English educated upper and middle class, emerged with high status. Unfortunately, these young men became misfits in the society. They had rejected the way of life, the values and the manner of dress of their fathers along with the traditional occupations that were still available. Their job aspirations, work experience and training were not compatible with an agricultural economy in which the number of white-collar jobs and occupations in industry was severely limited. In 1970, 55% of university graduates in Sri Lanka were without jobs. Most of them were graduates in liberal arts.

In 1971–77, 42% of those who committed suicide were in the 15–24 age group with a mean high rate of 42. The peak suicide rate occurred consistently in the 20–24 age group and the second highest rate in the 15–19 age group (Dissanayake and Padmal De Silva, 1983).

Mass media

Suicide in our society is a taboo subject. It helps to break down the taboos and talk openly about the subject. On the other hand, suicide is contagious. Retterstol (1993) reported that in the United States and West Germany, the suicide rates increased after the dramatic publication of suicide in the newspapers and showing of soap operas and television series in which suicide was the main theme.

The mass media without doubt have an important mission to perform with regard to suicide prevention. They can break down the taboos on the subject by providing sober and sound educational information and help people understand why people attempt suicide. People will then dare to talk about the subject and about their own suicidal ideas. When these ideas are exposed, relatives, friends, neighbours or work mates will be able to detect early warning signs of suicide and help and offer these people support and perhaps prevent suicide.

But publishing detailed descriptions and names of suicides in the press in a sensational manner must be avoided. In the community, there are many who harbour suicide ideas and make suicidal attempts. That this is prevalent is something which people are not aware of. Sensational coverage of suicide in the mass media seems to push these vulnerable young to commit suicide. This is because potential victims may identify with the seemingly intolerable life situations of the person who committed suicide and suicide may become a model for the potential victim to escape from a similar life situation. This kind of identification with people who commit suicide can induce a feeling of inevitability about one's own suicide that may be irresistible (Sacks and Eth, 1981).

There is, therefore, a need for public information and plenty of factual information on this topic. Public information campaigns in this are also vitally important. However, all these must be done in a discreet way.

Therefore, the media should exercise great prudence and restraint in news concerning suicide. To eliminate the role of imitation as a contributing factor for suicide, Pardes and Blumenthal (1990) have suggested that the press should:

1. Deromanticize stories about suicide.
2. Accompany media presentations with information about available sources of help.
3. Avoid the details of suicide method.

Suicide method can be contagious. In Singapore, 'copy cat suicide' does occur among the young.

Limitation of availability of lethal agents

Cantor (1990) has proposed that limiting access to lethal methods that are commonly used in suicide attempts could reduce their suicide rate.

In the United Kingdom, for example, Cantor (1989) reported that the suicide rate by carbon monoxide poisoning declined from 40% to less than 10% when the British converted their home heating method from a highly lethal coke gas to a natural gas of low lethality. In Australia, the placement of restriction on the quantity of hypnotic also resulted in a substantial decline in the suicide rate in that country between 1960 and 1980 (Oliver and Hertzel, 1973). Blumenthal (1988) and Shaffer et al. (1988) stated that the use of firearms since 1970 has become the primary method of suicide for younger persons of both sexes in the United States. According to Cantor (1985), 65% of all young suicides in the United States were committed with firearms. In fact, Cantor and Baume (1988) hypothesized that limiting accessibility to firearms would result in 20% less young suicides.

In Singapore (1990), about 70% young suicides jumped from high-rise flats. Like in Hong Kong, more young females (90%) than males (58%) preferred this method of suicide. Most of them jumped from the flats they lived in. Of those who jumped from their own high-rise flats, 75% jumped from the kitchens and 6% from the bedrooms. Architects from the Housing Development Board in Singapore should look into the possibility of redesigning the kitchens in such flats. Possibly, more barriers should be erected in the kitchens.

The other method commonly adopted by the young in Singapore is hanging. Unfortunately potential interventions regarding hanging per se seems limited.

Drug overdose may in future be a potential problem in Singapore. The advent of new antidepressants safer than the tricyclics present opportunities for practitioners to change prescribing habits for a high risk population. The selective serotonin re-uptake inhibitors (SSRIs) and other new antidepressants are considerably safer in overdose than the tricyclics (Cantor and Baume, 1988).

Education

The prevention of young suicide is not only 'dependent on the ability to identify populations at high risk' but also on the ability to 'offer interventions that modify these risk factors before suicide ensues' (Brent et al., 1988). Experts believe that young suicides could be reduced by as much as 20% through public education (Holinger, 1984).

1. Parents

Poor parenting, and poor communication and relationship between parents and their young are important factors found associated with young suicides in Singapore.

The effort of the parents is particularly important in the first few formative years of the child's life. Society ought to give mothers and fathers a better opportunity to be at home with the child in these important years. Parents must create for their young safe and pleasant environments in which the young can develop their personal talents in a positive and creative way (Kosky and Goldney, 1994).

Most parents in Singapore send their babies for medical checkups. However, the checkups have so far been restricted to physical health. There ought to be an opportunity at such checkups to give guidance on emotional problems. Most parents do not receive training in bringing up children or have an education in child psychology.

There has been an explosion in research on infant development during the past decade and much is learned about human beings and their emotional development (Shaffer and Bacon, 1989). This information can also be used to aid the young in labelling, understanding and communicating their feelings. Also, the teaching materials on depressive disorder and signs of self-destructive tendencies among the young should be collected. Education for parents on mental illness and the signs, symptoms and treatment of young who are potentially suicidal could have a great impact on the suicide rate.

Finally, a supportive family member who has the capacity to provide empathy, who is consistently available, and who can set limits and is able to gratify the young's needs for self esteem may offer the necessary ingredients to offset the family stress that may exist.

2. Peers

It has been reported that friends and peers can play an important role in suicide prevention by acting as a link between these suicidal young and the helping professionals. Often they may be the first to notice early warning signs or symptoms of suicide or self-destructive behaviour in the vulnerable young. They must be encouraged to make sure a responsible person is informed and immediate help for the vulnerable young is sought.

Training

1. Teachers

Good nurseries with good specialists to deal with children from difficult backgrounds will also have a preventive effect on suicidal behaviour later.

In schools, an understanding and warmhearted teacher can do much for his students if he knows how to assess them individually and treat them accordingly. It is particularly important that no one should be portrayed as a loser or as inferior if he does not perform well at school. Everyone has an area in which he can assert himself, whether it is languages, mathematics, arts, music or sports. The problem of 'losers' must be kept constantly in mind. They are to some extent victims of our efficient society.

School teachers should be trained to detect early depressive disorder or other severe mental illness in their pupils so that they may know when to refer them for further assessment or treatment.

Recreation, hobby and sport clubs and religous associations can be of great preventive value. The young need targets to work towards commitment and the possibility of self-realization.

Education to help the young to understand and to cope with emotional relationship and social problems is important. Developing ways of encouraging young to seek help in a crisis must also be given a high priority. Suicidology should be included in the teaching given in the school system.

'Screening protocol' for schools to detect early young with emotional problems and to identify young who are at risk of committing suicide should be devised so that the emotionally disturbed and potentially suicidal young can be detected and sent for early treatment. But most importantly, new ways of reaching out to these young with problems should be found.

2. Professional help groups

Many occupational groups such as ambulance staff, the fire brigade, police, prison, the clergy and the SOS may need special courses. They must be trained to have a correct attitude towards potential young suicide candidates and to cope effectively with such clients at times of emergency.

Training of professional help groups (paraprofessionals) in recognizing potentially young suicide is important. Finally, better training for health care professionals in managing and treating young in crisis should be implemented.

3. Medical professionals

Suicide can be prevented by upgrading the competence of medical professionals – physicians (especially medical practitioners), psychiatrists, psychologists, psychiatric nurses, social workers and counsellors – by increasing their knowledge of suicide, improving their interview techniques and skills, and teaching them when to make appropriate referral.

It is stated that suicide arouses anxiety in medical practitioners who often lack the skill to deal with suicidal patients because of ignorance. Michel and Valachi (1992) suggested that the medical practitioners' knowledge and attitude towards suicide could be influenced significantly by seminar discussions between medical practitioners and psychiatrists. Also, medical practitioners could be stimulated to increase their knowledge about the diagnosis and treatment of patients with depressive disorder by a lecture style education programme.

Increased knowledge of depressive disorder and its disguises is necessary for all general physicians and non-psychiatric specialists so that effective treatment can be instituted in time. It is also important for knowledge on medication to reach all doctors since experience has shown that there are doctors who use too low a dose of antidepressants. It was reported that the suicide rate dropped in the year after the programme was introduced.

Evaluation should include awareness that depressive disorder in children differs in presentation from adult-type of depressive disorder. Traditional depressive signs do not appear as frequently as they do among adults. Instead, the very young are more likely to become agitated or irritable or react in a negativistic fashion or become involved in behaviour that is troublesome to others (Federick, 1985). They may also present inefficiency in school.

Therapy

The range of therapy includes no-suicide contract, cognitive therapy, brief counselling geared to problem-solving, family approach and relevant pharmacological treatment. Interestingly, it has been shown that no one of the above therapy is found to be more superior to other (Aaronson et al., 1989).

In therapy, the guidelines for working with potential suicide victims are essentially the same as any for disturbed young people in general with the exception that the risk of suicide for them is much higher. Thus, therapy would begin:

> By establishing a dependency-gratifying relationship that is not threatening to the young. It would then proceed to stimulation of emotional growth within this relationship, including encouragement of increased self-sufficiency without stirring fears of abandonment. Finally, it would gradually diminish the dependent aspects of the relationship at a pace consistent with the young person's maturation, accepting that some patients will require a degree of support almost indefinitely. (Meeks, 1971).

The key to success is to be 'warm, caring, and responsive without being familiar or effusive' (Cantor, 1977). The young may be terrified, confused, embarrassed or humiliated. A simple handshake which conveys warmth, care and respect will help to alleviate these fears and put him at ease. Besides, this gesture of physical contact makes him feel at home. Try to remove the aura of omnipotence and distance.

The therapist must be involved and let the young know that he shares and hears his pain without blocking the flow of emotion. The therapist should want to be seen as a friend in a common struggle and as a source of wisdom. He must not pass judgment on what the young says.

Patience, an even disposition and humour are the prime requirements on the part of the therapist (Toolan, 1975).

The treatment of young is difficult because the young are frequently provocative and will often test the therapist's tolerance. The therapist is sometimes torn between sympathy for the young's despair and recognition of a realistic need for limit-setting, knowing that either course may lead to a suicidal act. Therapy with young often involves stormy periods. No therapist can help his client if he does not like him.

Some parents may collude with the young to deny the seriousness of the suicidal attempt. It is therefore important to see both parents and the young. The goal in seeing the parents is to help the family become aware of the underlying emotional configuration that provokes the destructive patterns and to seek remedies for potential change.

A young is often brought to treatment unwillingly (Nicholi, 1978). Thus, in the young's first visit, the therapist must establish enough of a communication to allow the young to want to come again. Each therapist develops his own method of accomplishing this elusive task. The young may be looking for someone whom he can trust and who will be consistent. He may, however, find the therapist too irrelevant, too formal, too inflexible and too unavailable.

In cognitive therapy, the therapists believe that if one thinks depressed one feels depressed, whereas more traditional therapists tend to believe that one who feels depressed will think depressed. The aim of cognitive therapy is mainly to correct the negative view the individual has of self, the world and the future. It is said that the directness of cognitive therapy may hold an extra appeal for adolescents (Bedrosian and Beck, 1979; Beck and Epstein, 1982).

In pharmacotherapy, there is a general clinical assumption that anti-psychotics, anti-manic and antidepressants should be as effective in young people with mental illness as they are in adults. Khuri and Akiskal (1983) have made a strong argument that energetic treatment and on-going follow-up of patients with primary and secondary affective disorders will prove to be an effective method of preventing suicide.

Working with chronically suicidal young can be extremely difficult. Burnout is a common experience among therapists who have to deal with several suicidal young at the same time. One of the ways to prevent burnout is to share the burden with others as much as possible. Periodic consultations with a respected colleague or regular supervision can be especially helpful. Motto (1985) reported that no therapist should handle more than three or four young suicidal patients at one time.

Should even one young at risk be turned away from a focus on death and towards a more meaningful life, the effort is worthwhile.

Hospitalization

Hospitalization is necessary if suicidal young are in danger of harming themselves or others, or if their families are not available, not supportive or disruptive.

A period of hospitalization has a number of advantages.

1. It can allow for a period of adjustment to medication and for the young to get engaged in therapy.
2. It can afford the therapist the time to evaluate the young and the family situation before making treatment plans.
3. It allows the parents a brief respite from their constant vigilance and worry about the suicidal young.
4. It can assure the young that his cries for help have been taken seriously and are not dismissed as an attention-getting manoeuvre.

On the other hand, hospital stay can be experienced as

depersonalizing and punitive. Among the costs of hospitalizing young are the isolation of the young from available supports, the reinforcement of dependency and the perceived stigma attached to the hospitalization per se.

If the hospital is not used, an extensive support system must be available. This includes frequent therapy appointments, very frequent telephone contacts, the cooperation of family and friends as well as the removal of lethal weapons from the house. Sometimes treatment requires removal of the young from a stressful to a non-stressful environment.

A young with suicide problems is also a young who shies away from contacting others. But he may be able to establish a relationship over the telephone. To be able to confide in someone over the telephone or discuss his problems in this way can be great relief for the troubled young. Telephone is a good means of communication. This source has not been sufficiently developed in the treatment and prevention of suicide of the young.

However, hospitalization while decreasing the risk of suicide, does not eliminate it. There is no evidence that hospitalization reduces longer-term suicide risk or that hospitalization is an effective treatment for suicidal behaviour per se.

Suicide prevention centres

There are suicide prevention centres all over the world. In Europe, ten years after the war, Erwin Ringel founded the suicide prevention centre in Vienna in cooperation with the Catholic Church and the Catholic Welfare organization. Their work formed the basis for the foundation of the International Association for Suicide Prevention.

During the last century, telephone services to help people in distress sprouted in various parts of the United Kingdom and the United States. In these two countries, the two main branches are the Samaritans and the Los Angeles Suicide Prevention Center respectively. It is said that the Samaritans befriend while thc American counsels.

The Samaritans of Singapore (SOS) was inaugurated in December 1969. They provide a 24-hour telephone service to help those in distress. Volunteers taken on are carefully screened. They are trained to listen, calm the callers, assess the problems and are taught when to refer their callers to the professionals. The SOS offers friendship, neighbourliness and care. Everything that is said is confidential. SOS also provides crisis counselling and an emergency service when requested by the police and their clients. SOS gives talks to the public. There is a panel of consultants to whom they may refer when necessary.

In Los Angeles, it was discovered that over 98% of the people who committed suicide had not contacted the Los Angeles Suicide Prevention Center (Weiner, 1969). The reasons given were lack of knowledge and inability to take action, fear, shame or other barriers such as cultural differences and languages. This centre formed the model for more than two hundred centres that gradually developed in the United States. It has been reported, however, that around a third of these centres are small and do not have any paid staff. There is, thus, a significant difference in quality in the various centres. Doubts have been expressed over the effectiveness of some of these centres.

Lester (1974) reported that there was no evidence that any of the centres specializing in telephone referral services had reduced the suicide rate. Instead, he warned that they were in danger of unknowingly providing inferior and dangerously low quality services unless maximum control over their 24-hour telephone answering service was maintained (Barraclough and Jennings, 1977; Jennings et al.,1978).

Miller et al. (1984), in a large study of whether such organizations and centres would decrease suicide rates found that such centres consistently reduced the suicide rates of only one group – young white females. They reported that there was a decline in suicide rates of 55% in countries in which crisis centres were established and an increase of 85% in those in which they were not. The authors also suggested that many lives might be saved if suicide prevention centres were generally available throughout the United States.

In conclusion, it is felt that suicide prevention centres, which provide 24-hour telephone consultation and service, do provide a service to those who are mentally distressed and do prevent young females in certain countries from committing suicide. However, such services manned by trained volunteers must be properly supervised and controlled. The leading centres also do have an enormous effect in furthering knowledge of suicidology. They promote educational activity and stimulate interest in suicide research.

References

Aaronson EL et al. (1989). Reluctance to help-seeking by adolescents. Paper presented at the Annual Meeting of the American Association of Suicidology, San Diego.

Ahmed O, Farouk L. (1983). Egypt. In: Headley LA, ed. *Suicide in Asia and the Near East*. Berkeley: University of California Press; pp 333–49.

Ahmed SH. (1983). Pakistan. In: Headley LA, ed. *Suicide in Asia and the Near East*. Berkeley: University of California Press; pp 258–71.

Anderson EN, jr. (1972). Some Chinese methods of dealing with crowding. *Urban Anthropology*; 1: 146–51.

Asberg M, Nordstrom P, Traskman-Bendz L. (1986). Biological factors in suicide. In: Roy A, ed. *Suicide*. Baltimore: William & Wilkins, pp 47–72.

Asberg M, Nordstrom P, Traskman-Bendz L. (1986). Cerebrospinal fluid studies in suicides: An overview. *Annal NY Academic Science*; 487: 243–55.

Banki CM et al. (1984). Biochemical markers in suicidal patients. Investigation with cerebrospinal fluid amine metabolites and neuroendocrine tests. *Journal Affective Disorder*; 6: 341–50.

Barraclough BM, Jennings C. (1977). Suicide prevention by the Samaritans. *Lancet*; ii: 237–9.

Barracloug BM. (1978). Reliability of violent death certification in one coroner's district. *British Journal of Psychiatry*; 132: 39–41.

Barraclough BM. (1987). *Suicide: Clinical and Epidemiological Studies*. Australia: Croom Helm Ltd., Provident House.

Bathia SC et al. (1987). High risk suicide factors across culture. *The International Journal of Social Psychiatry*; 33 (3): 226–36.

Beck AT, Schuyler D, Herman I. (1974). Development of suicide intent scales. In: Beck AT, Resnick HLP, Lettieri DJ, eds. *The Prediction of Suicide*. Maryland: Charles Press.

Beck AT, Kovacs M, Weissman A. (1975). Hopelessness and suicidal behavior: An overview. *Journal of the American Medical Association*; 234: 1146–9.

Beck AT et al. (1979). The measurement of pessimism: The hopelessness scale. *Journal Consult and Clinical Psychology*; 42: 861–5.

Beck AT, Epstein N. (1982). Cognitions, attitudes, and personality dimensions in depression. Paper presented to the Annual Meeting of the Society for Psychotherapy Research. Smuggler's Notch, Vermont.

Bedrosian RC, Beck AT. (1979). Cognitive aspects of suicidal behavior. In: *Suicide Life-Threatening Behavior*; 9: 87–96.

Berman AL. (1988). Fictional depiction of suicide in television film and imitation effects. *American Journal of Psychiatry*; 145: 982–6.

Blumentahl SJ. (1988). A guide to risk factors, assessment, and treatment of suicidal patients. *Medical Clinic North America*; 72: 937–71.

Blumenthal SJ, Kupfer DJ. (1988). Overview of early detection and treatment strategies for suicidal behavior in young people. *Journal of Youth and Adolescence*; 17: 1–23.

Brahams D. (1991). Suicide and attempted suicide: The legal implication. In: Montgomery SA, Goeting NLM, eds. *Current Approaches: Suicide and Attempted Suicide. Risk Factors, Management and Prevention*. Southampton Duphar Laboratories Ltd., pp 48–55.

Brent DA et al. (1988). Risk factors for adolescent suicide. A comparison of adolescent suicide victims with suicidal inpatients. *Archives of General Psychiatry*; 45: 581–8.

Brown G, Linnoila M. (1990). Cerebrospinal fluid serotonin metabolite (5–HIAA) studies in depression, impulsivity and violence. *Journal Clinical Psychiatry*; 51 (Suppl.): 31–4.

Bunney WE, Fawcett JA. (1965). Possibility of a biochemical test for suicide potential. *Archives of General Psychiatry*; 13: 232–9.

Bussaratid S, Ruangtrakool S. (1983). Thailand. In: Headley LA, ed. *Suicide in Asia and the Near East*. Berkeley: University of California Press, pp 143–66.

Calvin JF. (1985). An introduction and overview of youth suicide. In: Peck ML, Farberow NL, Litman RE, eds. *Youth Suicide*. New York: Springer Publishing Company, pp 1–16.

Cantor CH, Baume PJM. (1998). Access to methods of suicide. What impact? *Australian & New Zealand Journal of Psychiatry*; 32: 8–14.

Cantor P. (1975). The effects of youthful suicide on the family. *Psychiatric Opinion*; 12: 6–11.

Cantor P. (1989). Intervention strategies; Environmental risk reduction for youth suicide. In: *Report of the Secretary's Task Force on Youth Suicide. Vol 3: Prevention and Interventions in Youth suicide*. (DHHS Publ No ADM–89–1623). Washington, DC. U.S. Government Printing Office.

Cantor P. (1990). Symptoms, prevention, and treatment of attempted suicide, in depressive disorder: Facts, theories, and treatment methods. In: Wolman B, Stricker G, eds. *Depressive Disorders: Facts, Theories, and Treatment Methods.* New York: John Wiley, pp 189–202.

Cantor PC. (1977). Suicide and attempted suicide among students: Problems, prediction, and prevention. In: Cantor PC, ed. *Understanding a Child's World: Readings in Infancy Through Adolescence*. New York: Mcgraw Hill, pp 344–443.

Cantor PC. (1985). Testimony before United States Subcommittee on Juvenile Justice, Washington, DC.

Capstick A. (1960). Recognition of emotional disturbance and prevention of suicide. *British Medical Journal*; 1: 1179–82.

Carlson GA, Cantwell DP. (1982). Suicidal behaviour and depression in children and adolescents. *Journal of the American Academy of Child Psychiatry*; 21: 361–8.

Carrigan MS, Whittinghill JR, Derrick A. (1985). Psychological autopsy of completed suicide in children and adolescents. *American Journal of Psychiatry;* 142: 1061–4.

Carroll BJ, Greden JF, Feinberg M. (1982). Suicide, neuroendocrine dysfunction and CSF 5-HIAA concentration in depression. *Advance Bio-Science;* 31: 307–31.

Census of population, Singapore, 1957, 70, 80 & 90. Department of Statistics, Singapore.

Centers for Disease Control (CDC). (1988a). Recommendations for a community plan for the prevention and containment of suicide clusters. *Morbidity and Mortality Weekly Report*; 37: (Suppl. S-6): 1–11.

Chen CC et al. (1991). Aldehyde dehydrogenase deficiency, flush patterns and prevalence of alcoholism: An interethnic comparison. *Acta Medica Okayama*; 45: 409–16.

Chen AJ. (1969). Recent trends of deaths from unnatural causes (accident, suicide, homicide) in Singapore 1961–65. *Singapore Medical Journal*; 10 (2): 72–83.

Chia BH, Tsoi WF. (1972). Suicide in Singapore. *Singapore Medical Journal;* 13: 91–7.

Chia BH. (1978). Suicide in Singapore. MD thesis. University of Singapore.

Chia BH, Tsoi WF. (1979). Suicide letters. *Annal Academy of Medicine*; 3(3): 298–300.

Chia BH. (1981). *Suicidal Behaviour in Singapore*. Tokyo: SEAMIC (South East Asian Medical Information Center).

Chong MY, Yeh EK, Wen JK . (1992). Suicidal behaviour in Taiwan.

In: Kok LP, Tseng WS, eds. *Suicidal Behaviour in the Asia-Pacific Region*. Singapore: University Press, pp 69–82.

Chong MY, Cheng TA. (1995). Suicidal behaviour observed in Taiwan: Trends over four decades. In: Lin TY, Tseng WS, Yeh ED. eds. *Chinese Societies and Mental Health*. Hong Kong: Oxford University Press, pp 209–18.

Choprapawon C, Visalyaputra S. (1992). Suicidal behaviour in Thailand. In: Kok LP, Tseng WS, eds. *Suicidal Behaviour in the Asia-Pacific Region*. Singapore: Singapore University Press, pp 127–43.

Cosand BJ, Bourque LB, Kraus JF. (1982). Suicide among adolescents in Sacramento County, California 1950–1979. *Adolescence*; 17: 917–30.

DeCastro EF, Pimenta F, Martins I. (1988). Female independence in Portugal: Effect on suicide rates. *Acta Psychiatric Scandinavica*; 78: 147–5.

Dissanayake SAW, Padmal De Silva. (1983). Sri Lanka. In: Headley LA, ed. *Suicide in Asia and the Near East*. Berkeley: University of California Press, pp 167–209.

Dixon WA et al. (1992). Use of different sources of stress to predict hopelessness and suicide ideation in a college population. *Journal of Counselling Psychology*; 39: 342–9.

Djamour J. (1959). *Malay Kinship and Marriage in Singapore*. New York: Athlone Press.

Drake ER et al. (1984). Suicide among schizophrenics. Who is at risk? *The Journal of Nervous and Mental Disease*; 172 (10): 613–7.

Dunne EJ. (1992). Following a Suicide: Postvention. In: Bongar B. *Suicide: Guidelines for Assessment, Management and Treatment*. New York: Oxford University Press, pp 221–34.

Elkind D. (1967). Egocentrism in adolescence. *Child Development*; 38: 1025–34.

Ember CR, Ember M. (1985). *Cultural Anthropology*. Englewood Cliffs; Prentice Hall.

Fan MZ et al. (1992). Suicidal behaviour in China. In: Kok LP, Tseng WS, eds. *Suicidal Behaviour in the Asia-Pacific Region*. Singapore: Singapore University Press, pp 58–68.

Farberow NL (1989). Preparatory and prior suicidal behavioural factors. In: *Report of the Secretary's Task Force on Youth Suicide. Vol. 2: Risk Factors for Youth Suicide*. (DHHS Publ No ADM-89-1622). Washington, DC: U.S. Government Printing Office.

Federick CJ. (1985). An introduction and overview of youth suicide. In: Peck ML, Litman RE, eds. *Youth Suicide*. New York: Springer Publishing Company, pp 1–16.

General household survey, 1985: Socio-demographic and economic characteristics. Department of Statistics, Singapore.

Gist R, Welsh QB. (1989). Certification change versus actual behavior changes in teenage suicides rates 1955–1979. *Suicide and Life-Threatening Behavior*; 19: 227–87.

Godney RD, Burvill PW. (1989). Trend in suicidal behaviour and its management. *Australian & New Zealand Journal of Psychiatry*; 13: 301–7

Gould MS, Shaffer D. (1986). The impact of suicide in television movies: Evidence of imitation. *New England Journal of Medicine*; 135: 690–4.

Graham C, Burvill PW. (1992). A study of coroner's records of suicide in young people, 1986–88 in Western Australia. *Australian & New Zealand Journal of Psychiatry*; 26: 30–9.

Gutheil TG. (1984). Malpractice liability in suicide. *Legal Aspects of Psychiatric Practice;* 1: 1–4.

Gutheil TG. (1992). Suicide and suit: Liability after self destruction. In: Jacob D, ed. *Suicide and Clinical Practice*. Washington, DC. American Psychiatric Press, pp 147–68.

Hagnell O, Rorsman B. (1980). Suicide in the Lundby study: A controlled prospective investigation of stressful life events. *Neuropsychobiology*; 6: 319–22.

Hall JA. (1978). Gender effects in decoding nonverbal cues. *Psychological Bulletin*; 85: 845–58.

Hassan R, Tan KL. (1970). Suicide in Singapore: A sociological analysis. *South East Asia Journal of Society*; 3: 11–7.

Hassan R. (1983). *A Way of Dying: Suicide in Singapore*. Oxford: Oxford University Press.

Hassan R. (1987). Lives Unlived: Youth Suicide in Australia. Paper presented to Youth Suicide Conference, Prince Henry Hospital, Sydney, New Youth Wales.

Hassan R, Carr J. (1989). Changing patterns of suicide in Australia. *Australian & New Zealand Journal of Psychiatry*; 23: 226–34.

Hawton K. (1986). Suicide in adolescent. In: Roy A, ed. *Suicide*. Baltimore: William & Wilkins, pp 135–50.

Hawton K, Catalan J. (1987). *Attempted Suicide: A Practical Guide to its Nature and Management*. Oxford: Oxford University Press.

Haynes R. (1984). Suicide in Fiji: A preliminary study. *British Journal of Psychiatry*; 145: 433–8.

Haynes R. (1987). Suicide and social response in Fiji: A historical survey. *British Journal of Psychiatry*; 151: 21–6.

Headley LA. (1983). *Suicide in Asia and the Near East*. Berkeley: University of California Press.

Heim N, Lester D. (1990). Do suicides who write notes differ those who do not? A study of suicides in West Berlin. *Acta Psychiatrica Scandinavica*; 82: 372–3.

Hoberman HM, Garkindel BD. (1988). Completed suicide in youth. *Canada Journal of Psychiatry*; 33: 494–504.

Hoberman HM, Garkindel BD. (1989). Completed suicide in youth. In: Pfeffer CR, ed. *Suicide among Youth: Perspectives on Risk and Prevention*. Washington, DC: American Psychiatric Press, Inc., pp 21–40.

Holinger P. (1984). Suicide prevention and intervention. In: *Carter Center: Closing the Gap Project*, Atlanta, GA: Centers for Disease Control.

Holinger PC et al. (1994). *Suicide and Homicide among Adolescents*. London: Guilford Press.

Hoskin JO, Friedman MI, Cawte JE. (1969). A high incidence of suicide in preliterate-primitive society. *Psychiatry*; 32: 199–210.

Hsu J. (1985). The Chinese family: Relations, problems and therapy. In: Tseng WS, Wu DYH, eds. *Chinese Culture and Mental Health*. New York: Academic Press, Inc., pp 95–112.

Hughes DR. (1965). *The People of Malaya*. S'pore: Eastern Universities Press.

Hwu HG, Chen CC, Yeh EK. (1995). Alcoholism in Taiwan: The Chinese and aborigines. In: Lin TY, Tseng WS, Yeh EK, eds. *Chinese Societies and Mental Health*. Hong Kong: Oxford University Press, pp 181–96.

Iga M. (1970). Studies of social problems by Japanese scholars. *Rice University Studies*; 56 (4): 173–87.

Iga M, Tatai K. (1975). Characteristic of suicides and attitude towards suicide in Japan. In: Farberow NH, ed. *Suicide in Different Culture*. Baltimore: University Park Press, pp 255–80.

Igu M. (1981). Suicide in Japanese youth. *Suicide Life-Threatening Behavior*; 11: 17–30.

Jan O'Donnel, Farmer R, Catalan J. (1993). Suicide notes. *British Journal of Psychiatry*; 163: 45–8.

Jennings C, Barraclough BM, Moses JR. (1978). Have the Samaritans lowered the suicide rates? A controlled study. *Psychological Medicine*; 8: 413–22.

Kakar S. (1978). *The inner world: A Psychoanalytic Study of Childhood and Society in India*. Oxford: Oxford University Press.

Kato MS. (1969). Self destruction in Japan: A cross-cultural epidemiological analysis of suicide. *Foflia Psychiatrica et Neurologica Japonica*; 23: 291–307.

Kessler RC et al. (1988). Clustering of teenage suicides after television news stories about suicides. *American Journal of Psychiatry;* 145: 1379–83.

Khuri R, Akiskal HS. (1983). Suicide prevention: The necessity of treating contributory psychotropic disorders. *Psychiatric Clinical North America*; 6: 193–207.

Kleiman A. (1989). Patients and healers in the context of culture. Berkeley: University of California Press.

Kok LP, Aw SC. (1992). Suicide in Singapore, 1986. *Australian & New Zealand Journal of Psychiatry*; 26: 599–608.

Kok LP, Tseng WS. (1992). *Suicidal Behaviour in the Asia-Pacific Region*. Singapore: Singapore University Press.

Komos L, Bach E. (1985). Source of errors in registering suicide. *Acta Psychiatrica Scandinavica;* 71: 227–9.

Koocher PG. (1964). Talking with children about death. *American Journal of Orthpsychiatry;* 44: 404–11.

Kosky R. (1987). Is suicidal behaviour increasing among Australian youth? *Medical Journal of Australia*; 147: 164–6

Kotila L, Lonnquist J. (1987). Adolescents who make suicide attempts repeatedly. *Acta Psychiatrica Scandinavica;* 76: 386–93.

Kramer M et al. (1972). *Mental Disorders / Suicide*. Cambridge, MA: Harvard University Press.

Kua EH, Tsoi WF. (1985). Suicide in the island of Singapore. *Acta Psychiatrica Scandinavica;* 71: 227–9.

Kua EH et al. (1990). Drinking Problems. *Singapore Medical Journal*; 31: 247–9.

Lau BWK, Kung NYT, Cheung JTC. (1983). How depressive illness presents in Hong Kong. *Practitioner*; 227: 112–4.

Lee RPL. (1980). Perceptions and uses of Chinese medicine among the Chinese in Hong Kong. *Culture, Medicine and Psychiatry*; 4: 345–75.

Lee RPL. (1985). Social stress and coping behaviour in Hong Kong. In: Tseng WS, Wu DYH, eds. *Chinese Culture and Mental Health*. Orlando: Academic Press, Inc., pp 193–214.

Lee RPL. (1995). Culture tradition and stress management in modern society: Learning from Hong Kong experience. In: Lin TY, Tseng WS, Yeh EK, eds. *Chinese Societies and Mental Health*. Hong Kong: Oxford University Press, pp 40–52.

Lefkowitz MM, Tesiny EP. (1980). Assessment of childhood depression. *Journal Consult Clinical Psychology*; 48: 43–50.

Lester D. (1974). Effect of suicide prevention centers on suicides rates in the United States. *Health Services Reports*; 89: 37–9.

Lester D. (1990). Changes in the methods used for suicide in 16 countries from 1960–1980. *Acta Psychiatrica Scandivanica*; 81: 260–1.

Lester G, Lester D. (1971). Suicide: The gamble with death. New Jersey: Prentice Hall.

Lin TY. (1953). A study of incidence of mental disorders in Chinese and other cultures. *Psychiatry;* 16: 315–35.

Lin TY, Lin MC. (1982). Alcoholism among the Chinese: Further observations of a low-risk population. *Culture, Medicine and Psychiatry*; 6: 109–16.

Lin TY. (1985). Mental disorders and psychiatry in Chinese culture: Characteristic features and major issues. In Tseng WS, Wu DYH, eds. *Chinese Culture and Mental Health*. Orlando: Academic Press, Inc., pp 369–93.

Linkowski P et al. (1983). Thyrotrophin response to thyrostimulin in affectively ill women: Relationship to suicidal behaviour. *British Journal of Psychiatry*; 143: 401–5.

Lo WH. (1985). Suicide and attempted suicide in Hong Kong with a note on prevention. *Hong Kong Journal of Mental Health*; 14: 64–75.

Lo WH, Leung TM. (1985). Suicide in Hong Kong. *Australian & New Zealand Journal of Psychiatry*; 19: 287–92.

Lo WH. (1992). Suicidal behaviour in Hong Kong. In: Kok LP, Tseng WS, eds. *Suicidal Behaviour in the Asia-Pacific Region*. Singapore: Singapore University Press, pp 83–111.

Mahatir BM. (1970). *The Malay Dilemma*. Singapore: Federal Publication.

Marzuk PM, Tardiff K, Hirsch CS. (1992a). The epidemiology of murder-suicide. *Journal of the American Medical Association*; 267: 3179–83.

McCarthy PD, Walsh D. (1975). Suicide in Dublin: The under-reporting of suicide and the consequence for national statistics. *British Journal of Psychiatry*; 126: 301–8.

McIntyre MS, Angle CA. (1970). The child concept of death. Paper presented to The Workshop in Methodology, Atlantic City, Ambulatory Pediatric Society.

Mehta K. (1990). *Giving Up Hope: A Study of Attempted Suicide Amongst Indian Women*. Singapore: Times Books International.

Meeks J. (1971). *The Fragile Alliance*. Baltimore: Williams & Wilkins

Michel K, Valachi L. (1992). Suicide prevention: Spreading the gospel to general practitioners. *British Journal of Psychiatry;* 160: 757–60.

Miller HC, et al. (1984). An analysis of the effects of suicide prevention facilities in the United States. *American Journal of Public Health*; 74: 340–3.

Miller SE. (1979). The biosocial survey in Hong Kong. Canberra: The Australian National University. Centre for Resource & Environmental Studies.

Mingzhao F, Congpei L, Jeuiji W. (1992). Suicidal behaviour in China. In: Kok LP, Tseng WS, eds. *Suicidal Behaviour in the Asia-Pacific Region*. Singapore: Singapore University Press, pp 58–68.

Motto JA. (1970). Newspaper influence of suicide. *Archives of General Psychiatry*; 23: 143–8.

Motto J. (1985). Treatment concerns in preventing youth suicide. In: Peck ML, Farberow NL, Litman RE, eds. *Youth Suicide*. New York: Springer Publishing Company, pp 91–111.

Murphy GE. (1992). *Suicide in Alcoholism*. Oxford: Oxford University Press.

Nicholi Am jr. (1978). The adolescent. In: Nicholi AN, ed. *Harvard Guide to Modern Psychiatry*. Cambridge, MA: Harvard University Press, pp 519–41.

Nikkyo N. (1975). *The Richer Life*. Tokyo: Kosei Publishing Co.

Nikkyo N. (1982). *The Meaningful Life*. Tokyo: Kosei Publishing Co.

Oliver RG, Hertzel BS. (1973). An analysis of recent trends in suicide rates in Australia. *International Journal Epidemiology*; 1: 91–101.

Ong S, Yeoh KL. (1992). Suicidal behaviour in Kuala Lumpur, Malaysia. In: Kok LP, Tseng Ws, eds. *Suicidal Behaviour in the Asia-Pacific Region*. Singapore: Singapore University Press, pp 144–75.

Ots T. (1990). The angry liver, the anxious heart and the melancholic spleen. *Culture, Medicine and Psychiatry;* 14: 21–58.

Overstone IMK. (1973). A psychiatric approach to the diagnosis of suicide and its effect upon the Edinburgh statistics. *British Journal of Psychiatry*; 123: 15–21.

Pallis DJ et al. (1982). Estimating suicide risk among attempted suicide. 1. The development of new clinical scales. *British Journal of Psychiatry*; 141: 37–44.

Pallis DJ, Gibbons JS, Pierce Pw. (1984). Estimating suicide risk among attempted suicide. 1. Efficiency of predictive scales after the attempt. *British Journal of Psychiatry;* 144: 139–48.

Palmer S, Humphrey J. (1980). Criminal homicide followed by offender's suicide. *Suicide and Life-Threatening Behavior*; 10: 106–18.

Pardes H, Blumenthal SJ. (1990). Young suicide; Public policy and research issues. In: Blumenthal SJ, Kupfer DJ, eds. *Suicide Over the Life Cycle: Risk factors, Assessment, and Treatment of Suicidal*

Patients. Washington, DC; American Psychiatry Press, Inc., pp 665–84.

Petzel SV, Cline D. (1978). Adolescent suicide: Epidemiological and biological aspects. *Adolescent Psychiatry*; 6: 239–66.

Pfeffer CR. (1985). Observations of ego functioning of suicidal latency-age children. In: Peck ML, Farberow NL, Litman RE, eds. *Youth Suicide*. New York: Springer Publishing Company, pp 39–47.

Pfeffer CR. (1989). Life stress and family risk factors for youth fatal and nonfatal suicidal behavior. In: Pfeffer CR, ed. *Suicide Among Youth: Perspectives on Risk and Prevention*. Washington, DC: American Psychiatric Press, Inc., pp 143–64.

Phillips DP. (1982). The impact of fictional television stories on U.S. adult fatalities: New evidence on the effect of the mass media on violence. *American Journal of Sociology*; 87: 1340–59.

Phillips DP, Carstensen LL. (1986). Clustering of teenage suicides after television news stories about suicide. *New England Journal of Medicine*; 315: 685–9.

Phillips DP, Paight DJ. (1987). The impact of fictional television suicide stories on U.S. fatalities: A replication. *American Journal of Sociology*; 317: 809–11

Phillips DP, Carstensen LL. Paight DJ. (1989). Effects of mass media news stories on suicide, with new evidence on the role of story content. In: Pfeffer CR, ed. *Suicide Among Youth: Perspectives on Risk and Prevention*. Washington, DC: American Psychiatric Press, pp 101–6.

Piaget J. (1960). *The Child's Concept of the World*. New York: Littlefied Adams, Patterson.

Poteet DJ. (1987). Adolescent suicides: A review of 87 cases of completed suicide in Shelby County, Tennessee. *American Journal Forensic Medical Pathology;* 8: 12–7.

Raleigh VS, Bulusor L, Balragan R. (1990). Suicide among immigrants from Indian subcontinent. *British Journal of Psychiatry*; 156: 46–50.

Raleigh VS, Balarajan R. (1992). Suicide and self burning among Indians and West Indians in England and Wales. *British Journal of Psychiatry*; 161: 365–8.

Rao AV. (1983). Indian. In: Headley LA, ed. *Suicide in Asia and the Near East*. Berkeley: University of California Press, pp 210–37.

Remafedi G, Farrow J, Deisher R. (1991). Risk factors for attempted suicide in gay and bisexual youth. *Pediatrics;* 87: 869–75.

Retterstol N, Ekeland H, Heso R. (1985). Suicide among the young: development in Norway. A 7-year study from Oslo. *Tidsskr. Nor. Laege Foren*; 105: 119–22.

Retterstol N. (1993). *Suicide: A European Perspective*. Cambridge: Cambridge University Press.

Rin H. (1975). Suicide in Taiwan. In: Farberow NL, ed. *Suicide in Different Cultures*. London: University Park Press, pp 239–54.

Rin H, Chen T. (1983). Taiwan. In: Headley LA, ed. *Suicide in Asia and the Near East*. Berkeley: University of California Press, pp 59–86.

Rosaldo MZ, Lamphere L. (1984). *Women, Culture, and Society*. Stanford: Stanford University Press.

Rosen BK. (1981). Suicide pacts: A review. *Psychological Medicine*; 11: 525–33.

Roy A. (1986). Suicide in schizophrenia. In: Roy A, ed. *Suicide*. London: Williams & Wilkins, pp 92–112.

Roy A. (1989). Genetic and suicidal behavior. In: *Report of the Secretary's Task Force on Youth Suicide. Vol 2: Risk Factors of Youth Suicide*. (DHHS Publ No ADM-89-1622). Washington, DC: U.S. Government Printing Office.

Roy A. (1989). Genetics and suicide behaviour. In: Pfeffer CR, ed. *Suicide Among Youths: Perspective on Risk and Prevention*. Washington, DC. American Psychiatric Press, pp 165–84.

Rudd MA. (1989). The prevalence of suicidal ideation among college students. *Suicide and Life-Threatening Behaviour;* 19: 173–83.

Sacco W, Graves D. (1986). Correspondence between teacher ratings of childhood depression and child self-ratings 1985. *Journal of Clinical Child Psychology*; 4: 353–5.

Sacks M, Eth S. (1981). Pathological identification as a cause of suicides on an inpatient unit. *Hospital Community Psychiatry*; 32: 36–40.

Sathyavathi K, Rao DLNM. (1961). A study of suicide in Bangalore. *Trans All India Institute of Mental Health*; 2:1.

Sathyavathi K. (1976). Male and female suicide in Bangalore: A longitudinal study over a ten year period. *Trans All India Institute of Mental Health*; 10: 105.

Schmidt CW et al. (1977). Suicide by vehicular crash. *American Journal of Psychiatry;* 134 (2): 175–8.

Schonert KA. (1992). Sex differences in moral reasoning among emotionally disturbed adolescents. In: Feinstein S, ed. *Adolescent Psychiatry: Developmental and Clinical Studies*. Chicago: University Chicago Press.

Schuckit MA, Schuckit JJ. (1989). Substance use and abuse: A risk factor in youth suicide. In: *Report of the Secretary's Task Force on Youth Suicide. Vol 2: Risk Factors for Youth Suicide*. (DHHS Publ

No ADM-89-1622). Washington, DC; U.S. Government Printing Office.

Schulsinger R et al. (1979). A family study of suicide. In: Shou M, Stromgren R, eds. *Prevention and Treatment of Affective Disorder*. New York: Academic Press.

Schweitzer R, Klayich M, LcLean J. (1995). Suicidal ideation and behaviour among university students in Australia. *Australian & New Zealand Journal of Psychiatry;* 29: 473–9.

Seward J. (1968). *Hara-kiri: Japanese Ritual Suicide*. Tokyo: Charles E. Tuttle Company.

Shaffer D. (1974). Suicide in childhood and early adolescence. *Journal Child Psychological Psychiatry*; 15: 275–92.

Shaffer D, Fisher P. (1981). The epidemiology of suicide in children and young adolescents. *Journal of American Academy Child Psychiatry*; 20: 545–65.

Shaffer D, Gould M, Braubman P. (1985). Paper presented to Conference on the Psycholobiology of Suicidal Behavior, New York.

Shaffer D, Gould M. (1987). A study of completed and attempted suicides in adolescents. *Progress Report*, Rockville, MD: NIMH.

Shaffer D. (1988). The epidemiology of teen suicide: An examination of risk factors. *Journal of Clinical Psychiatry*; 49: 36–9.

Shaffer D et al. (1988). Preventing teenage suicide: A critical review. *Journal of the American Academy of Child and Adolescent Psychiatry;* 27: 679–80.

Shaffer D, Bacon K. (1989). A critical review of preventive efforts in suicide, with particular reference to youth suicide. In: *Report of the Secretary's Task Force on Youth Suicide. Vol 3: Prevention and Interventions in Youth Suicide*. (DHHS Publ No ADM-89-1622). Washington, DC: U.S. Government Printing Office, pp 31–61.

Shafii M et al. (1985). Psychological autopsy of completed suicide in children and adolescents. *American Journal of Psychiatry*; 142: 1061–4.

Shafii M. (1989). Completed suicide in children and adolescents: method of psychological autopsy. In: Pfeffer CR, ed. *Suicide Among Youth: Perspective on Risk and Prevention*. Washington, DC: American Psychiatric Press, Inc., pp 1–19.

Shear M, Frances A, Weiden P. (1983). Suicide associated with akathisia and depot fluphenazine treatment. *Journal of Clinical Psychopharmacology*; 3: 235–6.

Shek DTL. (1993). Adolescent suicide in Hong Kong. Paper presented to the World Psychiatric Conference, Tokyo, Japan.

Shen YC. (1987). Recent epidemiological data of alcoholism in China. *Chinese Mental Health Journal;* 6: 251–6.

Shen YC et al. (1981). Investigation of mental disorders in Beijing suburban district. *Chinese Medical Journal*; 94 (3): 153–6.

Shneidman ES. (1976). Suicide notes reconsidered. In: Shneidman ES, ed. *Suicide: Contemporary Development*. New York: Grune & Stratton, pp 253–78.

Singer K, Wong M. (1973). Alcoholic psychoses and alcoholism in the Chinese. *Quarter Journal Study alcohol*; 34: 878–86.

Singer K. (1975). Depressive disorders from a transcultural perspective. *Social Science and Medicine*; 9: 289–301.

Snowden J. (1989). Suicide in Australia: A comparison with suicide in England. *Australian & New Zealand Journal of Psychiatry*; 13: 301–7.

Strue FA. (1986). Clinical electroencephalography and the study of suicide behavior. In: Maris R, ed. *Biology of Suicide*. New York: Guilford Press, pp 51–86.

Suk JH. (1992). Suicidal behaviour in Korea. In: Kok LP, Tseng WS, eds. *Suicidal Behaviour in the Asia-Pacific Region*. Singapore: Singapore University Press, pp 41–57.

Tamney JB. (1969). The reality of religious labels: A study of religion among Singapore University Students. In: Hassan R, Tamney JB, eds. *Analysis of an Asian Society*. Singapore: Department of sociology, University of Singapore.

Tanaka-Matsumi J, Marsella AJ. (1976). Cross-cultural variations in the phenomenological experience of depression. 1. Word association studies. *Journal of Cross Cultural Psychology*; 7: 379–96.

Tatai K. (1983). Japan. In: Headley LA, ed. *Suicide in Asia and the Near East*. Berkeley: University of California Press, pp 12–58.

Taylor JB. (1975). *Thinking about Islam*. London: Butterworth Educational.

Taylor EA, Stansfied SA. (1984). Children who poison themselves. II. Prediction of attendance for treatment. *British Journal of Psychiatry;* 145: 132–5.

Teoh JE. (1974). An analysis of completed suicide by psychological postmortem. *Annal Academy of Medicine*; 3 (2): 117–24.

Thompson TR. (1987). Childhood and adolescent suicide in Manitoba: Demographic study *Canada Journal of Psychiatry*; 32: 264–9.

Toolan JM. (1962). Suicide and suicidal attempts in children and adolescents. *American Journal of Psychiatry;* 118: 719–24.

Toolan JM. (1975). Suicide in children and adolescents. *American Journal Psychotherapy*; 29: 339–44.

Trautman PD. (1989). Specific treatment modalities of adolescent suicide attempters. In: *Report of the Secretary's Task Force on Youth Suicide. Vol 3: Prevention and Interventions in Youth Suicide*. (DHHS Publ No ADM-89-1623). Washington, DC: U.S. Government Printing Office, pp 253–63.

Tsu TWT. (1966). *Your Chinese Roots: The Overseas Chinese Story*. Singapore: Times Books International.

Tu A. (1981). Examination pressure. In: Khoo TP, ed. *Aspects of Mental Health Care*, Hong Kong. Hong Kong: Mental Health Association of Hong Kong.

Tuckman J. Kleiner RJ, Lavell M. (1959). Emotional content of suicide notes. *American Journal of Psychiatry*; 116: 59–63.

Ward BE. (1970). Temper tantrum in Kau Sai; Some speculation upon their effects. In: Mayer P, ed. *Socialization: The Approach from Social Anthropology*. London: Tavistock.

Wasserman IM. (1984). Imitation and suicide: A reexamination of the Werther effect. *American Sociology review*; 49: 427–36.

Wee V. (1976). Buddhism in Singapore. In: Hassan R, ed. *Singapore: Society in Transition*. Kuala Lumpur: Oxford University Press.

Weiner IW. (1969). The effectiveness of a suicide prevention program. *Mental Hygiene*; 53: 357–63.

West DJ. (1966). *Murder Followed by Suicide*. Cambridge: Harvard University Press.

Yap PM. (1958). *Suicide in Hong Kong*. Hong Kong: Oxford University Press.

Yeh EK, Hwu HG, Lin TY. (1995). Mental disorders in Taiwan: Epidemiological studies of community population. In: Lin TY, Tseng SW, Yeh EK, eds. *Chinese Societies and Mental Health*. Hong Kong: Oxford University Press, pp 247–65.

Yoshimatsu K. (1992). Suicidal behaviour in Japan. In: Kok LP, Tseng WS, eds. *Suicidal Behaviour in the Asia-Pacific Region*. Singapore: Singapore University Press, pp 15–40.

Yufit RI. (1989). Developing a suicide screening instruments for adolescents and young adults. In: *Report of the Secretary's Task Force on Youth and Suicide. Vol 4: Strategies for Prevention of Suicide*. (DHHS Publ No ADM-89-1624). Washington, DC: U.S. Government Printing Office.

Index